CHOSEN

Cheryl Lynn Carter

Cheryl Lynn Carter

© Cheryl Lynn Carter 2023

ISBN: 9798854746281

Cover design by Cheryl Lynn Carter

All rights reserved. No part of this publication may be reproduced in part or in whole in any format whatsoever without first contacting the author for permission.

Contents

Foreword

Introduction

Chapter 1 – Ariel School

Chapter 2 – Falcon Lake

Chapter 3 – Pascagoula

Chapter 4 - Rendlesham Forest

Chapter 5 – Mario Woods

The Edge of Enigma

Foreword

The mystery of alien encounters and abductions continues to elude conventional explanations. As someone who has spent time studying this phenomenon, I am constantly reminded of the intricacies and complexities of these experiences. During my time as a UFO/UAP researcher I have encountered a plethora of accounts that challenge our understanding of reality and stretch the boundaries of our perception.

Throughout history, there have been accounts of strange encounters with non-human entities, often described as gods, angels, or otherworldly beings. These experiences are not limited to specific cultures or time periods, but rather, span across different continents and epochs. From ancient myths and folklore to modern-day reports, the underlying theme of contact with beings from beyond our world persists.

The phenomenon is not limited to physical sightings of unidentified flying objects (UFOs), but also encompasses a wide range of experiences, including encounters with non-human beings, altered states of consciousness, and anomalous events that defy conventional explanations. It is important to approach the phenomenon with an open mind and a

Chosen

multidisciplinary perspective while drawing on insights from fields such as psychology, sociology, anthropology, and parapsychology.

Among the myriad of experiences that fall under the umbrella of alien encounters, the phenomenon of abduction stands out as a particularly perplexing enigma. Abduction experiences typically involve the alleged physical contact and abduction of individuals by non-human beings, often described as "gray" aliens with large black eyes. These accounts often share common characteristics, such as the sensation of floating or being levitated, the feeling of paralysis, and encounters with otherworldly environments or technologies.

One of the most intriguing aspects of the phenomenon of alien encounters and abductions is the reported phenomenon of missing time. Many witnesses claim that during their encounters, they experienced a period of time that they cannot account for, as if their memories were erased or altered. This phenomenon has been described as a "time slip" or a gap in consciousness that cannot be easily explained by conventional means.

Cheryl Lynn Carter

The phenomenon of abduction cannot be easily dismissed as mere hallucinations or hoaxes. The accounts of abductees are often detailed and vivid, with a consistency of themes and motifs that transcend cultural and geographical boundaries. Many abductees report similar experiences, despite having no prior knowledge of the phenomenon or exposure to popular media representations. These accounts cannot be simply reduced to psychological or physiological explanations, but rather, demand a deeper exploration of the nature and purpose of these alleged abductions.

It is possible that the phenomenon may not be solely physical in nature, but rather, involve interactions with other dimensions or realities beyond our own. Non-human entities reported in abduction experiences may not be extraterrestrial beings from distant planets, but rather, entities from other dimensions or parallel universes that coexist with our own.

It could be speculated that these entities may not be bound by the laws of space and time as we understand them, but rather, possess advanced abilities to manipulate our perception of reality.

The societal stigma associated with people sharing such experiences can also lead to isolation and ostracization, with witnesses often feeling compelled to keep their encounters a secret for fear of ridicule or disbelief.

Will we learn the truth behind the mystery? Time will tell. Until then, there are plenty of excellent researchers such as Cheryl Lynn Carter searching for the answers to the ongoing enigma.

When reading this book, I ask that you keep an open mind and be willing to challenge your preconceived notions and beliefs.

Vinnie Adams
Disclosure Team and UAPMEDIAUK

Introduction

Consciousness is described as perceptual awareness or higher-order thought. Further study of consciousness reveals the possibility of human interaction with non-human intelligence. Those who have had encounters or experienced abduction know this to be true.

In some cases, it is evident that this non-human intelligence is aware of our very thoughts sometimes before they are realized. Moreover, there is the probability they may be capable of inducing thoughts into our mind making one believe these thoughts are our own. Experiencers maintain they are fully capable of suppressing thoughts leaving a gap in our consciousness.

These non-human entities transversing the space-time continuum sometimes afford us glimpses of other realities; glimpses that may leave one wondering, why was I …

CHOSEN

Chapter 1
The Ariel School Encounter

During the night of September 14, 1994, between the hours of 10:50 and 11:05 p.m. there were numerous sightings of a bright capsule shaped fireball with trailing fire passing through the sky of southern Africa. Meteorologists reported it was most likely a meteor or the re-entry of the Zenit-2 rocket from the Cosmos 2290 satellite launch.

Zimbabwe Broadcasting Radio 702 encouraged people to call in and describe what they witnessed. The general consensus was the object being the size of a plane, red-orange in color, with three huge lights at the front, and ten smaller lights behind. One witness stated there was an almost black center with fourteen lights flashing around it. Many thought it was something not of this world.

In the early morning of September 16, 1994, an unidentified flying object traveling across the Atlantic at unbelievable speed was pinged by Mexican radar. Shortly afterward, radar operators at O.R. Tambo International Airport in Johannesburg, South Africa observed an unidentified object and tracked it to a location near the Zimbabwe border by Ruwa. Two Air Force jets attempted to chase the object that they described as shiny. However, it eluded them traveling at twice the speed of sound.

In 1994, Ruwa, Zimbabwe, located about fourteen miles south-east of Harare the capital, was little more than a crossroads in a small agricultural region. Here was the Ariel Primary School, an educational foundation both multicultural and co-educational with grades 1-7, had a mission to promote a relevant, high quality curriculum for its students.

Ariel School

On the morning of September 16, 1994 at 10:15 a.m. sixty-two children went out for recess as the teachers were having their weekly staff meeting. The only other adult there was Alyson Kirkman who had volunteered to operate the Tuck Shop where they sold snacks. It was just a typical day for the children with their wide-eyed innocence until something happened that would change their lives forever. As the children ranging in age from 6-12 years looked up to see bright flashes of colored lights in the sky, they were not prepared for what was to happen next.

Through the bright lights, a strange glowing object appeared. It hovered in the sky with four small objects flying around it. The small ones had flashing flights that went from blue to purple, and then red. The silver disc-shaped craft with flashing red lights landed in a field on the hill about three hundred feet behind the school yard. As the children watched in amazement, three small humanoid figures disembarked from the craft. Curious, some of the children hurried to the edge of the school yard in order to see what was happening. At the edge were large logs preventing them from crossing into an area with gum trees and wild overgrown Savanna grass where there might be snakes or wild animals.

The strange visitors were described as three feet tall, wearing tight black clothing, with long necks, narrow white face, and large black oval eyes. One walked around a sort of walkway on the craft while one stood guard next to it.

Another appeared to move in a strange motion as it began to float into the school yard. It would be there, disappear, reappear a few feet closer, disappear, and then reappear again.

Some of the children hurried into the Tuck Shop telling Alyson Kirkman about a small man with a band around his head running around the schoolyard. Upon hearing this, Alyson was totally skeptical thinking the real motive was to get her outside in order to take snacks in her absence.

Upon approaching the children, some claimed the being had direct eye contact with them and communicated telepathically through its eyes. It conveyed messages; messages that young children couldn't quite equate with the world they knew. The being appeared very concerned about the future of our environment and wanted the children to understand how precious our planet is. One girl had a vision of the Earth after all the trees were gone. A boy had a vision of polluted oceans, but was told that because they were young they could still prevent bad things from happening. Another girl felt that time stood still during the interaction. She wanted to run away to be with her younger siblings, but was unable to break eye contact with the being.

The event lasted about fifteen minutes before, with a blink of the eye, the being was back on the other side of the fence and reentering the craft along with the others. Then it rose straight up into the sky and flew away at a high rate of speed.

The children wasted no time running into the school to report the strange visitors that were in the school yard. However, when the teachers went outside there was nothing to see that would collaborate their story so the day went on as usual … but how could it be?

Map indicating the distance from the school yard to the landing site; 243 yards

After school, the children some excited and others confused, went home to share the details of the incident with their families hoping to be believed and perhaps given help to understand. However, their story was not as well-received as they had hoped. How despairing it must have been being confronted by something they did not understand only to have been met with disregard. This left some of the children sad, thinking they had imagined everything, and had gone totally mad.

Headmaster Colin Mackie began to get inquires from some concerned parents as to what had occurred. "I believe the children did feel they saw something that we're not common with. But to actually say it was a UFO, I would be reluctant to make that decision."

The Investigation

Headmaster Colin Mackie contacted Tim Leach, the BBC chief correspondent stationed in Zimbabwe and Head of the Foreign Correspondents Association. Upon hearing about the incident, he was very eager to film and interview the children. He phoned his friend Cynthia Hind, MUFON Director and Field Investigator in Zimbabwe. She had recently interviewed people who had observed the strange lights in the sky on September 14 and felt the Ariel incident could be related. As a journalist in her own right, she published the "UFO AfriNews" booklets that chronicled events of UFO encounters and abductions.

Tim Leach				Cynthia Hind

They made arrangements to visit the school on Monday in order to document the interviews with the children and teachers. She contacted Headmaster Colin Mackie asking if he could arrange to divide the students into small groups so that they could draw what they had seen before everyone had a chance to discuss it with each other.

On September 19, at 12:00 p.m. the children and teachers were seated at tables in the staff room. As they patiently waited to begin, the atmosphere in the room was filled with both excitement and confusion. There would be no school curriculum followed that day because the topic could not be found in an elementary school text book. Soon Tim Leach and the BBC film crew arrived along with Cynthia Hind and her friend Gunter Hofer. During this time, Tim Leach also faxed the BBC about a possible link with the unidentified flying object observed across southern Africa and the craft the children had seen.

Gunter Hofer first came to learn about Cynthia Hind when his father had brought home a book called "UFOs: African Encounters." Shortly after reading the book, he was talking with his Grandmother and the subject of UFOs came up. He was quite amazed to hear that she had observed one in 1968 while standing outside her shop. Realizing that this phenomenon was real, he began his journey into Ufology. He remembered there was an address on the back of the book; the address of Cynthia Hind. He wrote to her saying he might be able to assist with her MUFON agenda and she invited him to a talk at her home. As an amateur astronomer and astrophotographer he could help identify possible confusion with any astronomical events such as bright planets, meteors,

Chosen

and satellites which were visible and often mistaken for UFOs. He was very good with electronics and made a device for her that would detect electro static which is said to be found near UFO landing sites.

Gunter Hofer

Tim Leach and Cynthia Hind looked over the nearly forty drawings the children had created beforehand. With crayon and paper, they had done their best to portray images of what they had experienced that day. The drawings depicted age appropriate, but detailed images of a craft and the beings. They then began the process of interviewing the children individually. Tim Leach felt it must be difficult for the children to experience something they could not quite explain while at the same time not being believed by the adults.

Having been a war correspondent did not prepare him for what he was about to hear. As words were spoken, stories were shared about innocence lost. He found the entire experience deeply unsettling.

"I could handle war zones, but I could not handle this." He was so affected by the stories that he felt the children needed guidance. He reached out to Dr. John E. Mack at Harvard specializing in Child Psychiatry to see if he could help. He stressed the fact in his letter that "This is for real."

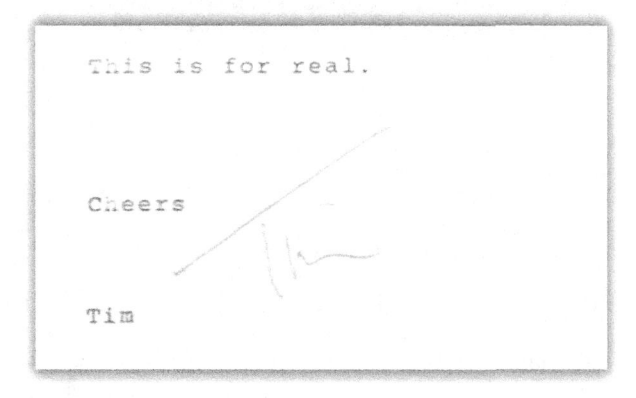

> This is for real.
>
> Cheers
>
> Tim

Last page of his letter to Dr. John E. Mack

Chosen

Through Their Eyes

The core of the children's narratives was remarkably consistent with them describing saucer shapes and beings with large black eyes. Leach noticed that some of the children's drawings were labeled "Thursday." When he asked the children about this, they said there had been strange objects in the sky the previous day, but didn't tell anyone. Thursday's object unlike the saucer shaped one on Friday was cigar shaped with flashing lights. It was observed flying above the power lines at the other end of the play ground. Then it disappeared only to reappear somewhere else before completely vanishing.

Leach continued the interviews with the children, expressing their own unique emotions, and discovered not all of them thought the beings were extraterrestrial. Some because of their cultural background had a different interpretation. It might have been a Zvikwambo, a spirit conjured by a witch doctor in order to drain the life out of a person or the Tokoloshe, an evil goblin that comes in the dark of night to steal the souls of humans. Thoughts like these seemed more surreal than the idea that extraterrestrial beings had visited them.

Cheryl Lynn Carter

Cynthia Hind Interviews

Cynthia Hind began looking over the various images the children had drawn; images that were drawn with such emotion. One particular drawing pulled at her heart strings as the young artist captured the horrified looks on the student's faces. The caption read: "I went out to break. I saw the alien. The children were scared."

Drawing by student witness capturing
the horrified looks on student's faces.

Brian R. age 12: "I saw a thing glinting by the tree and a door."

John W. age 11: "It was silver in the trees and it had landed on the ground. It had lights around it which were flashing. It was like a mirror, it reflected in the sun. And we looked at it closely and saw that it was in the shape of two saucers placed one on top of the other and it was silver."

Barry Downing age 11: "First I saw the crowd at the end of the playground; then I saw the object myself. It was surrounded by a ring of flickering lights, then a bright light lit up, and the object disappeared, and instantly reappeared somewhere else. This happened three times. Then something that looked like a small black bullet descended and landed near the gum trees. Some children saw a little man who appeared on top of the object dressed in black with a long, thin neck, and eyes like Rugby balls. The little man vanished and reappeared while we were seized by a breath of wind."

Fungai Mavengare age 12: Saw two little men who climbed off the object and walked to and fro before the children's eyes as if they were puzzled. Their movements looked like slow motion.

Guy Gibbons age 12: He was playing in the schoolyard when the excited shouting and gathering of his fellow students made him aware of "something going on." He went there and saw "this round object on the ground and some smaller ones next to it." Fascinated, he watched the object and a little man climbed out and walked around. The man was the size of a sixth grader. He had long, straight, black hair, and wore a tight fitting black suit. His eyes were extremely large and somewhat slanted. "He had but a slim slot for a mouth. I couldn't see a nose. While I was watching this, two of the smaller girls started to cry. I walked up to them and asked why they were crying. They said they were afraid the little man might come and eat them." Apparently they thought the being was a Tokoloshe." When he heard that, he got frightened too. When he went home, his parents wouldn't believe him. "There was no way to convince them. I can't help it. I can only keep it all for myself."

Cheryl Lynn Carter

The Field Investigation

After talking with the children, Gunter Hofer realized there had been two landing sites on two consecutive days, Thursday and Friday. He drew a map indicating each site and the proximity from the playground.

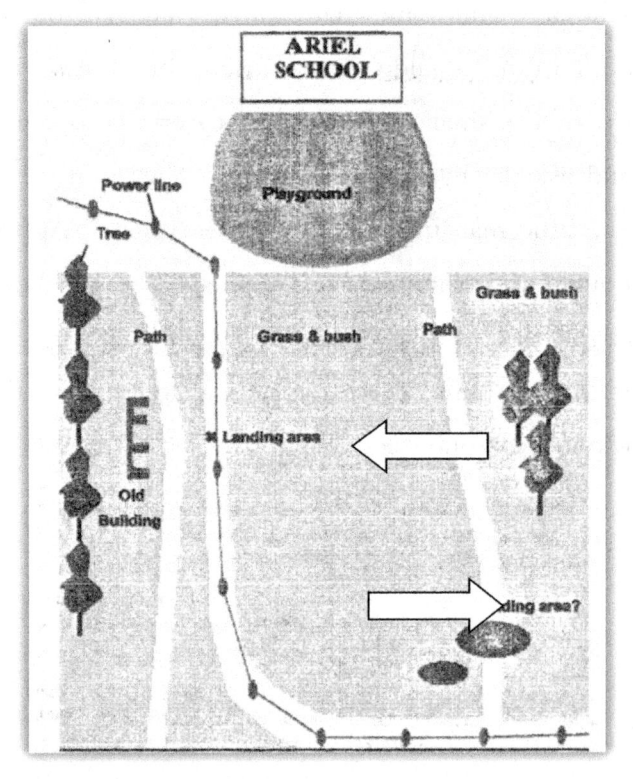

Map of the two Landing Sites

Chosen

Cynthia, two children Guy Gibbons and Fungai Mavengare, and Gunter Hofer headed over to Friday's landing site. Armed with an EMF meter, Geiger counter, and metal detector, Gunter began searching the landing site for evidence. They discovered the ground to be very hard and without grass, but no evidence was found.

Next they went to the grassy area on the other side of the fence on the playground. The boys were certain that a craft had landed between the third and fourth pole of the overhead power line on Thursday as depicted in the drawing.

Barry D. drawing of crafts flying over the power lines.

Tertia Nel

Gunter discovered two oval shaped areas of flattened grass that were about thirty feet long. Within the oval swirl of grass was a wedge-shaped impression in the dry soil as though something had pushed in. That was quite interesting as the ground at the time was very solid due to a long drought in Zimbabwe. Ground samples were sent to the University of Zimbabwe and they were found to contain only minor radioactive anomalies.

Wedge in the ground © Gunter Hofer

Chosen

Swirled grass © Gunter Hofer

Dr. John E. Mack

Dr. John Edward Mack was a Professor and Head of Psychiatry at the Harvard Medical School and an award-winning author. He risked his credibility with his colleagues by coming forward to say he believes the experiences of abductees are very real. When he had first encountered the phenomenon, he was skeptical. The idea that humans could be contacted by some other-worldly intelligence that could actually enter our world and have physical and emotional effects seemed unbelievable. At the time when he was invited to the Ariel School he was proposing to take a trip to Africa to investigate the possibility of abductions there. Having the opportunity to interview the children was of tremendous importance.

Together with his research associate Dominique Callimanopulas and Gunter Hofer who was invited back, they spent two days interviewing the children at length. Gunter had drawn a picture of the being that one of the boys described as wearing something similar to a wet suit and gave it to John Mack.

© Drawing of a being by Gunter Hofer

His insight with child psychiatry was very fundamental during the interviews and it enabled many suppressed memories to surface. Some were reluctant to speak so he gave each child personal space so they would feel safe and trust him. With all things considered, it was evident the children were telling the truth because their tone of voice and body language were consistent.

He also spoke to Headmaster Colin Mackie, the teachers, and some parents. He expressed the importance of listening and thinking about what the children were saying whether they believed them or not. It would be counter-productive to accuse them of not telling the truth because after all whatever happened was very real to them.

Headmaster Colin Mackie   Dr. John E. Mack

Dominique Callimanopulas

Mackie: "The one thing I've told everybody is we are dealing with children here. Sometimes the imagination can get carried away with them. We had one child who was very upset by the whole thing. Unfortunately, he's not at the school anymore.

Chosen

He's gone back to Canada. He was having sleepless nights. This is a 13 year old child. Basically the cause of that are his parents who refused to discuss the situation with him. According to them, this sort of thing doesn't happen."

Zara de Veron: 'I personally believe the children. They came running up here in such a panic. And I mean even if we had staged it, they could not have run all together like that. Even if we'd practiced it I don't know how many times. We were in a staff meeting and we just heard the screaming … screaming. Then they were here, you know. And a child can't make that up."

Zara de Veron

Mr. Mpofu: "We had staff meeting and the children were out by themselves. The children were quite excited …

shouting … quite a fright. At first I didn't believe it. There were people talking about UFOs that had been around and that have been seen. I thought it was just one of their imaginations. But later, the consistence and reports made me change my mind. I feel they saw something. Something really happened. They said things about these funny looking people who had just come to this school. They must have seen some of these aliens actually."

Mr. Mpofu

Leah Hwacha: "Some kids in my class are so frightened. I actually can see that. It must have affected them so much that they sort of imagine something will happen to them. They're still young. You don't know how to act and how to speak to them. You're a bit careful."

Judy Bates: "I live here at the school so I try not to think about it at all. I've had a lot of sleepless nights since it happened so I try to put it out of my mind ... Seeing is believing. I don't know, but then I'm scared of the unknown so it's something that I block off because I'd rather get on with school. I think the children are telling the truth, but I'd rather not think about it. Again because if I think about it, tonight I'll have another sleepless night cuz I'm waiting for an alien to come through the walls."

Judy Bates

He spoke with three children that had left the playground to venture into the thicket in order to get close to the object:

"We saw several beings and could look directly into the eyes of one of them. There was a large spaceship with some sort of a saucer on top of it, and there were some smaller spaceships hovering above the ground, and they were surrounded by small lights. When looking at them, they would look greenish. And they had some kind of a green window, but you wouldn't be able to see anything behind it. It was as though they had dark sun shades. The little objects were all gathering around the large spaceship."

"I saw two aliens. One was standing in front of the spaceship. He had a longish face, eyes, and two holes, but no nose. They had normal arms and legs. I saw one of these men by the spaceship. It was as if he was guarding the large spaceship and another one ran around and walked around in the grass. He walked staggering and didn't seem to be going anywhere. He just walked around. And then he ran again, but only a short way, and returned to the ship, and disappeared. Then the ship lifted off for about one meter and disappeared, and the little ones as well."

"I saw this hovering object, and it was quite big, and there were little ones all around it. It looked as though they were changing the spaceship. The beings from the spaceship walked into different directions. But it only looked like that … they walked … out there … those were strange beings. I saw one of them in particular; other children saw more of them. Some children were crying and I gave solace because there was nothing to worry about these beings. I don't know why I said this. People were crying, I turned around to see whether they were still there, and I saw this being. It had big black eyes and a black body. It was in front of the spaceship between the spaceship and us. It was slightly taller than me. It stood there and stared at me and Selma who had called the people to come here. It stared at us and we tried not to look into its eyes because that frightened us. His large eyes frightened us. It was as if he wanted to tell me, 'I want you. I want you to come with me.' My eyes followed him, my thoughts ... part of me wanted to follow him, but I was afraid. Something told me that I shouldn't go with him and something said that I wanted to go with him. I think they want people to know that we are making harm on this planet and that we mustn't get too technologic. That came to my head when the being looked at me."

Lisel Pillay age 11: "I saw several lights light up about at the height of the dam on the other side of the swamp. Suddenly, we saw a strange silver thing. My friends and I ran to see what it was. It was round, like a half of a plate. Then we saw somebody get out. He wore a black suit. His skin tone was bright and he was quite short. The eyes were pointy. I didn't see its nose nor mouth, but the eyes were very big. They were black. He seemed to be looking at all of us. I was frightened because I had never seen such a person before. First I thought it was the gardener, but his eyes were so big. My friend thought it was a UFO. He had long, black hair. He stood next to the ship. There was a second one who was walking around in slow motion. And there were smaller ships hovering around the big one. There were some. They appeared and disappeared. I saw them and then I didn't. The person looked sad. I felt sympathy, but also I was afraid. I felt sorry for him because I think he couldn't feel my love … that he needed love … I thought the world was gonna end, and that they had come to tell us that the world is gonna end … some kind of bad news … because we don't look after the planet properly and destroy the air. I felt horrible when I got home. I thought the world was gonna end and there would be no air to breathe. He never said anything, but his eyes looked horrible and something about his eyes told me this."

Trisha Nell age 12: "We saw a bunch of children gathering in one corner of the playground and Amy came and hailed us to come along to look at what it was. It was simply a shiny object over there in the bush. All the children said they had seen aliens, and stuff like that, but the teachers only said, 'Forget it, there was nothing.' I didn't see aliens or anything like that. I am afraid I was too far away. There was only a shiny object and there were many lights all around it."

Emily Windrom age 11: "I also only saw this really shiny object in the brush. Everybody was standing around it, like Trish said. Two girls saw it first and asked us to hurry and there was this glowing thing in the bush over there. It was somehow round at the bottom and the flat."

Tertia Nel age 11: "The day before the spaceship came, my friends and I were sitting in the playground. One of my friends, her name is Emily, looked up into the sky and said, 'Oh there's a UFO.' And I looked at it and she said, 'No, just kidding, it's an aeroplane.' And we looked up and um, I thought to myself, that can't be an aeroplane because it was very shiny. It looked like a cigarette, you know. It was a long thing and then on the end, it was all shiny. So I said maybe it is a UFO. So we're all kind of scared now and then the day that it happened, we started thinking, yeah that must have been a UFO in the sky because my brother Luke also saw it.

Amy Candas age 12: "My friends Claire, Hailey, and Camilla, and I strolled across the schoolyard when we saw this lunar-colored thing hover, appear, and disappear. And we followed it, and got onto one of those logs, and we looked, and saw this silver thing; it was shiny. We wanted to run there, but Claire said we mustn't. But I said it wouldn't be that bad, so we went closer to it, and saw this silver thing. At first we thought it could be a house up on the rock with reflecting glass or silver roof, but that was impossible because there simply was no house up there. We waited for some minutes and then we heard a flute sound. We went closer and I saw that black person moving as if in slow motion. I didn't want to see it, turned away, and as I looked again, it was gone."

Claire Rickson age 12: "We were in the schoolyard and saw a reddish light glittering in the msasa trees, and as it appeared and disappeared, we went down there. And we saw a big, white, silver burning object directly aside of the rocks, and we saw aliens in tight fitting black suits, their faces were not covered, who seemed to walk around in slow motion. You couldn't really see the ship because it was one huge light. But it was real. I was afraid and excited both at once. The being in the grass looked at me and we were terrified, and we ran back because we were afraid. And I was very angry with our teachers who wouldn't believe us."

Hailey age 12: It had a sliver thing that was down across the bottom. The noise that we heard in the air was like somebody playing a flute. I was afraid. I ran away from it. We told the teacher, but she said to forget about it. They weren't frightened of us. They actually came near."

Emma Kristiansen age 12: It was scaring myself. I saw a little object hovering. It was quite big actually and then there was little ones all around it. I saw this person and it had big eyes. That's all I saw about it, big eyes. But I was looking straight into his eyes. My heart kind of went faster, and then slower, and then faster, and then slower all at the same time … excitement and scariness. Happy because I saw something strange and something peculiar and something nobody had ever seen. The other man, his eyes looked at me as if uh, 'I want you to come with me. I want you to come.' Only my eyes went with him. It felt scary and a little excited, and a little like I shouldn't go. And yet, I want to go."

Two boys age 10: "We saw a silver thing over there near the trees. We had a long break and we were not allowed to go down the beaten path. The thing landed and stood there maybe two or three minutes. Then two or three people appeared who stood around the thing. It was like a comic. That thing had four legs and was quite big, and three people came out. They were wearing black suits and had big black eyes. They had landed on an ant hill and finally that thing lifted off again, approximately twice as high as I am tall, and then it disappeared … it simply disappeared."

Robyn Selous age 11: "It was during our long break and everybody was playing. Suddenly everybody came together, everybody ran there, me too. Everybody was afraid, so was I. I saw that thing that had landed in the trees and lights were shining. It was as if it had landed in the trees. It wasn't perfectly round, but rather oval, and the top was domed, it wasn't flat. And lights went all around it. Doors or anything like that were not visible. My friends said they had seen three things come out, with round faces. I didn't see them. I didn't go any closer. I cried and didn't know what was happening. I was so afraid that I locked myself in at the girls' room. I was afraid they were coming to fetch us. The teachers wouldn't believe us. They asked us to paint a picture of what we had seen and so we did. They still wouldn't believe us. I was so afraid I couldn't tell my mother about it."

Nataniel Coxall age 12: "It was silver and there was a ring of red lights around it. It was hovering above the trees. That's when I saw the two little men. Both of them were running. One was running in the trees and the other was running across the ship. They had on a black suit. They had short legs, a big head, and eyes bigger than ours. I would say that most of the kids in my class saw it as well."

Chosen

"Sometimes the worse place to be is in your head."

Some of the children claimed they never saw anything that day. Or perhaps they found it too painful to express. Unfortunately, some of them would never be the same even as they reached adulthood. They found it difficult to comprehend because there was nothing to compare this to and there may never be. Sometimes the worse place to be is in your head. Many are still impacted and some suffer from PTSD reliving the incident over and over wondering why they had been chosen.

Others are finally finding the courage to raise their voices and share the visions they received while looking into the black eyes of the mysterious beings so many years ago.

Emily Trim, like many others, was not able to talk to her family about what had happened as her missionary parents did not believe such things. After the incident in hopes of leaving this far behind, they removed her and two siblings from the school and moved back to Canada. But how is someone supposed to forget something that's so deep inside; so deep you can feel it in your soul?

Emily became an expressionist artist and through her paintings captured her inner thoughts, struggles, and silent despair over what she had encountered that day. One of her paintings portrays a little girl wearing pigtails that has her mouth zipped up; a sort of self-portrait. Today, Emily is proud to say that little girl is no longer afraid to speak.

Emily Trim speaking at the Alien Cosmic Expo 2015
Photo of her in the 3rd grade

Chosen

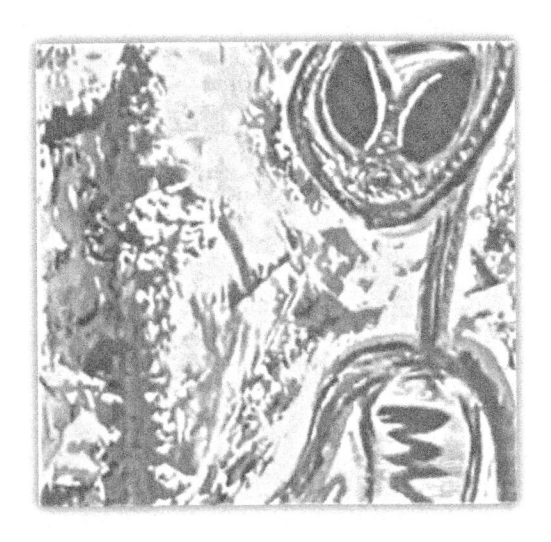

Emily: "Who cares what the ship looks like? Who cares where it landed? Who cares if it left a mark where it landed? All that matters is what they are saying to us."

Dr. John E. Mack: "There is a species that's out there that's more evolved. The big question is what are they doing? That's what we need to know so we can understand where we fall in their plan or whatever their ideas of the Universe are!"

———————————

Cynthia Hind "The Children of Ariel School Case #96, UFO AFRINEWS Issue #11, February 1995 ufoafrinews.com

Michael Hesemann "The Ruwa Incident: Part One" Magazine 2000 plus #118, May 1997

Gunter Hofer -Ariel School UFO Case Investigator Interview with Vinnie Adams - Disclosure Team - 2021

"Ariel Phenomenon: This Is Their Story" - Documentary Director Randall Nickerson - 2022

Chapter 2
Falcon Lake Encounter

Stefan Michalak, born in Poland, was a Captain in the Polish Army during the outbreak of World War II. With the defeat of the Polish Army after the German invasion, he joined the Polish Home Army. Also known as the Polish Underground, this was a dominant resistance movement in German occupied Poland. Here he operated as a partisan successfully participating in clandestine operations. During this time, he met Maria and they married in 1946. In 1947, the Allied occupation forces in Germany were concerned for his safety and assisted him in immigrating to Canada via the USS Virginian. Unfortunately, he was forced to leave behind his wife, daughter, and unborn son. Upon arriving, he began using Stephen as the spelling of his name and worked as a hired hand on a farm in Saskatchewan while continuing to struggle to bring his family to Canada. In 1957, they were finally united and a second son was born. Stephen moved the family to River Heights, Winnipeg, Canada where he began working as an Industrial Mechanic and became interested in geology.

The small resort town of Falcon Lake in Manitoba, Canada is about forty-seven miles north of the United States border in the rocky edge of the great Canadian Shield; the oldest shield on Earth composed of igneous bedrock from its volcanic history. The resort is situated near the southern edge of Whiteshell Provincial Park. The park, about the size of the state of Rhode Island is largely uninhabited wilderness and contains veins rich in silver and quartz deposits just waiting to be discovered. In 1966, after studying at the Saskatchewan prospecting school, Stephan's interest in geology grew and he filed several claims in order to prospect.

During Victoria Day weekend, he decided to do more prospecting in the Whiteshell Provincial Park, named after the megis snail shell sacred to the Ojibwe people, as he had previously filed promising claims including W10053. On May 19, 1967, after completing his shift at the Inland Cement Company where he was an Industrial Mechanic, he traveled by bus to Falcon Lake. He spent the night in room 17 at the Falcon Motor Hotel on the Trans-Canada Highway.

The following morning at 5:30 a.m., he headed north down the highway making his way into the bush and pine forest. He carried a briefcase of equipment: notebook, geology book of Manitoba, magnet, compass, gloves, protective welding goggles, hatchet, chipping hammer, steel tape measure, and raw porcelain used to check the formation for streak and color. By 9:00 a.m. it was a cloudless day and

Chosen

he located an area near a bog along Falcon Creek that was of particular interest to him because of the unique rock formation. He was hopeful that he would locate some more of the special specimens that he had found during a previous trip. He had momentarily startled some geese, but they soon settled down. Wearing his cap backwards because of the welding goggles, he slipped on his gloves and began chipping away. He momentarily stopped around 11:00 a.m. to eat the lunch his wife had packed: some smoked sausage, cheese, bread, an apple, two oranges, and coffee and then continued to explore the vein.

Stephen Michalak's quartz vein
© University of Ottawa Archives and Special Collections
Ontario Canada

At 12:15 p.m. while kneeling down and chipping away at some quartz, his attention was redirected to the geese that appeared to be agitated again. He looked up, noticed a light, and observed two cigar-shaped objects surrounded by a reddish glow descending from the south-west at an angle of 20 degrees above the horizon. As the objects grew closer, they appeared to be more oval shaped. The object further away stopped in mid flight and hovered about twelve feet above the ground while the other continued to descend landing on a large, flat rock outcropping about 160 feet away from him. The object that had been silently hovering approximately 15 feet overhead for about three minutes began to change from red to orange and then grey while ascending. Then it departed to the west at a high rate of speed before disappearing behind the clouds.

The object on the ground began to change colors from red to grey, until it turned the color of iridescent, hot stainless steel and was surrounded by a golden glow. Since Falcon Lake is near the U.S. border he believed this might be a secret U.S. Air Force project. Being a former military intelligence officer, this piqued his interest so he sat back for the next half hour, observed, and sketched it. The craft was saucer-shaped, about 60 feet in diameter, and about eight feet high with the dome an additional three feet high. There were no distinguishing markings on it.

His attention focused on an opening near the top of the craft where a brilliant purple light was streaming out. The light was so bright that it hurt his eyes. Soon he began feeling waves of warm air and detected the smell of sulfur.

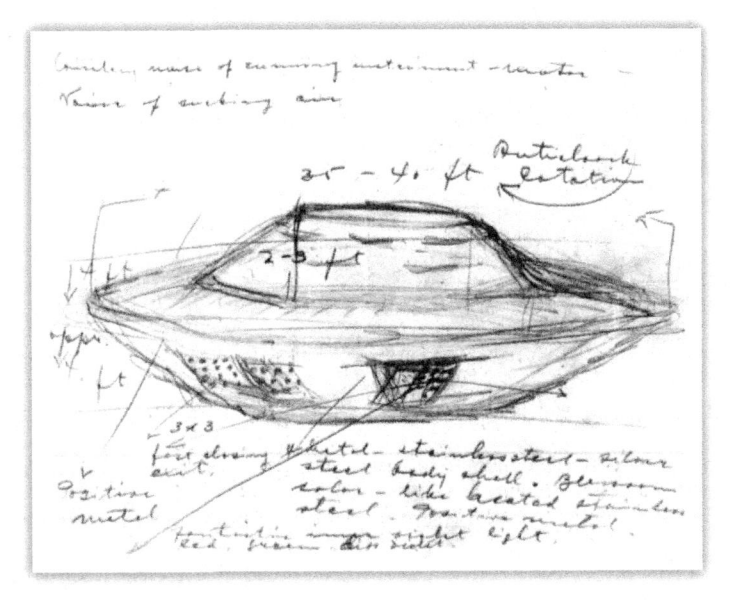

Drawing of the craft by Stephen Michalak
© University of Ottawa Archives and Special Collections
Ontario Canada

Suddenly, a hatch opened on the side of the craft. Confident in his military prowess he decided to move closer.

There didn't appear to be any identifying U.S. Air Force insignia. When he was about 60 feet away, he heard the whirling sound of a small motor.

As he listened, he heard two voices and other sounds coming from inside. Still convinced it was a secret experimental American craft that was perhaps in need of assistance he called out, "Okay, Yankee boys, having trouble? Come on out and we'll see what we can do about it," in English, but there was no response. He tried Russian, German, Italian, French, and Ukrainian, but still no response. Then the voices went silent.

Stephen approached the craft, placed the green lenses down on his goggles and stuck his head inside. There he observed panels with clusters of colored lights flashing in a random order, walls that were about twenty inches thick, and beams of light in horizontal and diagonal patterns. However, he did not see any occupants so he backed up and waited. Moments later, two panels slid across the door opening and a third dropped down from above completely sealing the opening. He noticed a small grid pattern on the side that could have been a sort of ventilation system measuring nine inches high by six inches wide with a uniform pattern of round holes that were 1/16 inch in diameter.

Chosen

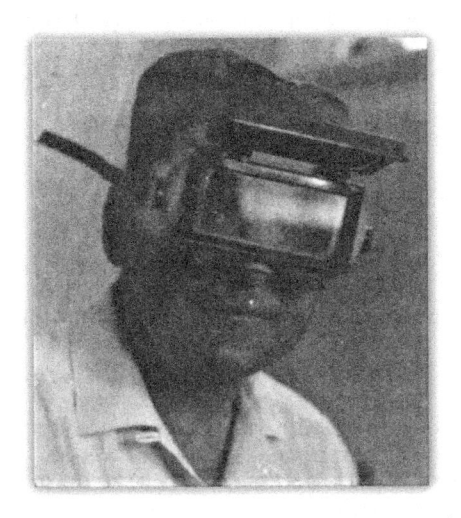

Welding goggles he wore while looking into the craft.
© University of Ottawa Archives and Special Collections
Ontario Canada

Once again he approached the craft. Upon examining the surface with his gloved hand, he found it be hot to the touch and constructed of a highly polished material with no welding or seams. The surface was so polished that it appeared to be like colored glass with light reflecting off it. Pulling his glove away, he realized three fingers of the glove melted and his fingertips were burned. Suddenly, the craft began to turn slightly to the left and a beam of heat shot out. Immediately, he felt a scorching pain on his forehead, around his chest, and realized his shirt and undershirt were on fire. Instinctively, he tore them away, and stomped on them so they wouldn't cause a brush fire.

The craft ascended into the sky, began turning red to orange, and was clocking speed far exceeding any aircraft he had ever seen. It headed to the west, the same direction as the other one, and quickly disappeared.

Stephen walked over to where he had left his equipment and noticed the compass needle was spinning erratically as if there was a magnetic disturbance. He began to get a headache so he quickly gathered up his equipment and put it inside his briefcase. Before leaving, he walked back to the landing site to look around. The lichen and moss that covered the rocks was blown off and piled in a circle about 15 feet in diameter. Suddenly, his headache became worse, he broke out in a cold sweat, was seeing colored spots before his eyes, and he began to feel nauseous. As he continued to feel weak and dizzy, he decided it best to head back to the motel.

Disoriented and nauseous, he stumbled through the forest eventually finding his way back to the road. As he breathed, a terrible sulfur odor was coming from his lungs. At 3:00 p.m. while on Highway 1 about a half mile west of the Falcon Beach entrance, Cst. G.A. Solotki of the Royal Canadian Mounted Police observed him on the side of the road trying to wave him down. Cst. Solotki approached him, but Stefan shouted for him to stay away.

Chosen

When Cst. Solotki asked why, Stephen who was very upset replied that he didn't want to expose anyone to radiation. When asked for his identification, he presented a document pertaining to prospecting with his name and address. Cst. Solotki inquired about the details of his experience leading up to him thinking he had been exposed to radiation.

Stephan related his story about seeing two space ships that glowed red and when he touched one he got burned. He showed Cst. Solotki his cap which the officer could see was burnt. When he asked to see his shirt, Stephen refused and backed away. There was a black substance on his chest which looked like ashes that he could have possibly rubbed on himself. Again, he backed away when Cst. Solotki tried to get a better look. He claimed to be in the area prospecting, but had no camping equipment only a briefcase similar to a Government Issue briefcase. When asked where the site was located, he stated he didn't want any publicity. The officer noted his general appearance was like that of one who had been abiding; red eyes and the inability to answer questions coherently. He asked if he could drive him to Falcon Beach, but he declined.

Cheryl Lynn Carter

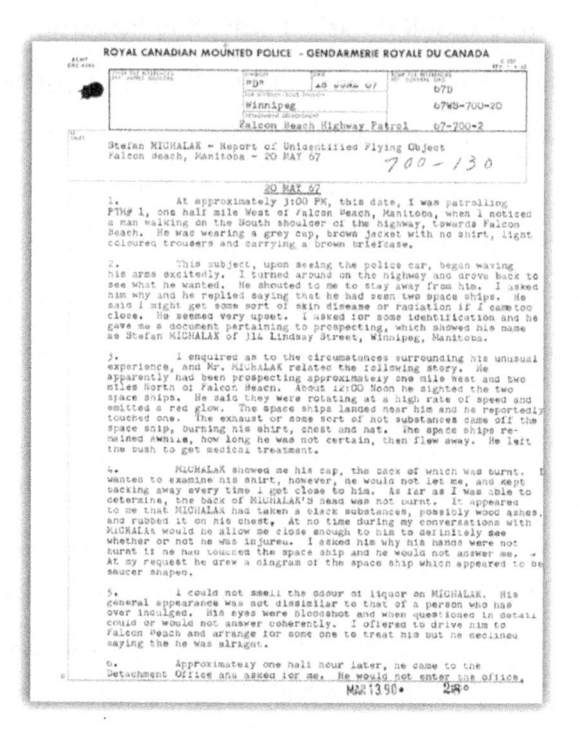

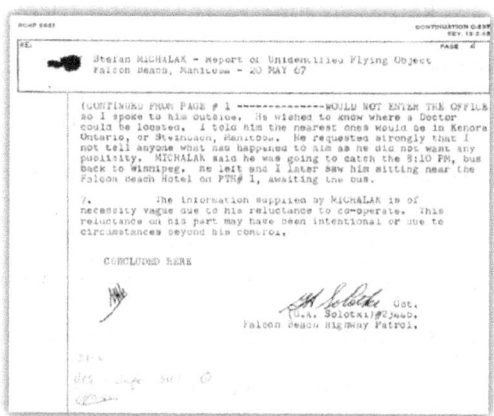

May 20, 1967 Report by Constable G. A. Solotki
www.baclac.gc.ca/eng/discover/unusual/ufo/documents/1967-06-18-Hwy.pdf

Chosen

Eventually, around 4:00 p.m. he was able to make his way back to the hotel. He approached Mrs. Buseck the wife of the hotel owner and inquired about locating a doctor. She said there wouldn't be a doctor available until July 1 and that he should go see the Royal Canadian Mounted Police if he needed help. He asked if he could make a collect call and she pointed to a pay phone. He phoned his wife saying there had been an accident, but everything was okay. He asked if she could arrange for their son Mark to meet him at the bus terminal. Then he waited several hours for the bus back to Winnipeg.

At 10:45 p.m. the bus arrived and his son took him directly to Misericordia Health Center where he experienced nausea, a headache, cold sweats, and an offensive odor coming from his lungs. He was examined and treated for first degree burns to his chest and stomach. These burns later turned into raised red sores in the form of a grid-like pattern like on the craft. His body smelled of sulphur and his symptoms pointed to radiation exposure. Since the hospital, he was attended by their family physician Dr. R. Douglas Oatway who examined him trying to determine why he had a loss of appetite and was not able to hold food down. He was prescribed medication for his headaches and to calm him down. He also was examined by Dr. S.S. Berger a skin specialist and by Dr. T.D. Cradduck who scheduled an appointment for a whole-body radiation scan at the National Atomic Research Centre in Pinawa, Manitoba in order to measure gamma radiation from isotopes in the body. The test results showed no count above normal.

There were several theories among doctors as to what had caused the burns. Some thought it had been the result of ultrasonic waves or thermal reaction caused by a blast of hot air under pressure. Radiologists believe it was the result of nuclear fission or the presence of gamma rays. Stephen contends that it was of his own doing as he stood so close to the craft making contact with the exhaust as it lifted off.

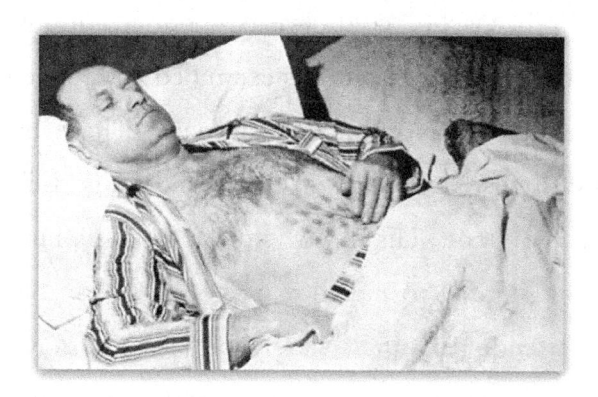

Grid-like pattern burns on his chest
© University of Ottawa Archives and Special Collections
Ottawa Canada

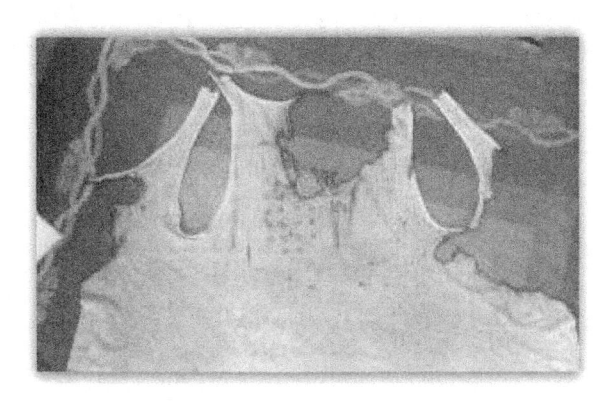

Chosen

A grid can be seen on his burned shirt
© University of Ottawa Archives and Special Collections
Ontario Canada

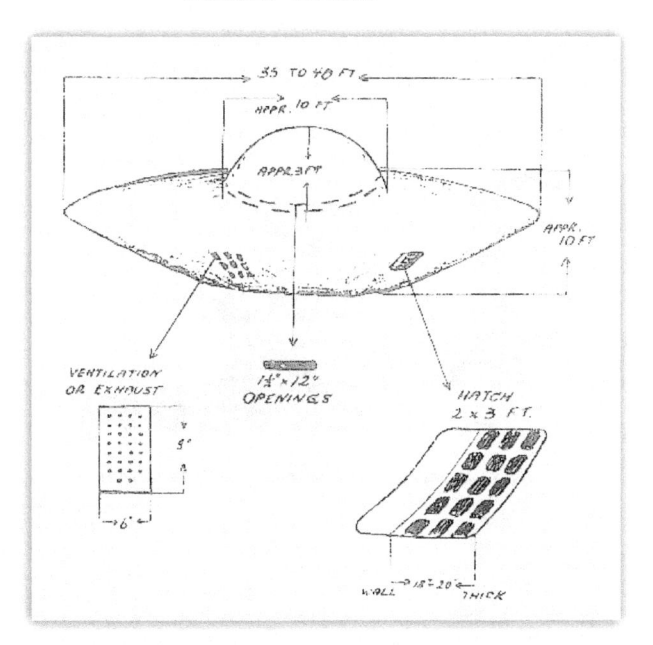

Pictorial description of the craft, hatch,
and the vent as described by Michalak.
© University of Ottawa Archives and Special Collections
Ontario Canada

Cheryl Lynn Carter

Winnipeg Tribune Interview

On Monday, May 22, he met with Peter Warren the Editor of the Winnipeg Tribune and Staff Writer Heather Chrisvin at the St. Regis Hotel to share his story. If this story was indeed true, Warren didn't want a rival newspaper to print it first. So he asked him to draw the craft he had seen. Without hesitation, Stephen sketched a very detailed likeness. Convinced this was real, he broke the incredible story on the front page.

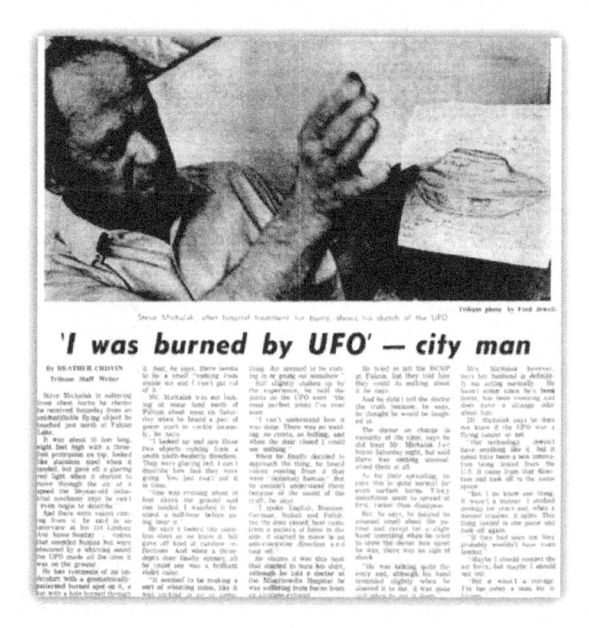

Front page of the Tribune May 22, 1967

Soon the news began to spread, the telephone would ring nonstop, and there was a continuous flash of reporter's cameras on his front lawn. Stephen Michalak was totally exhausted wanting only to distance himself from the outside world. "They could not know how I felt nor appreciate what I was going through. They just couldn't know."

Chris Rutkowski Interview

Chris Rutkowski lived down the street from Stephen Michalak. At the time, he was studying astronomy at the University of Manitoba and worked at the observatory. He would act as a field investigator whenever somebody had a UFO story. He would later become a science writer and Canada's most well-known Ufologist. Stephen Michalak's encounter was of great interest to him. After hearing his credentials, Stephen Michalak agreed and on May 24, 1967, he interviewed Stephen at great length at his residence. At last Stephen felt that somebody was trying to understand what he was going through.

Cheryl Lynn Carter

Chris Rutkowski

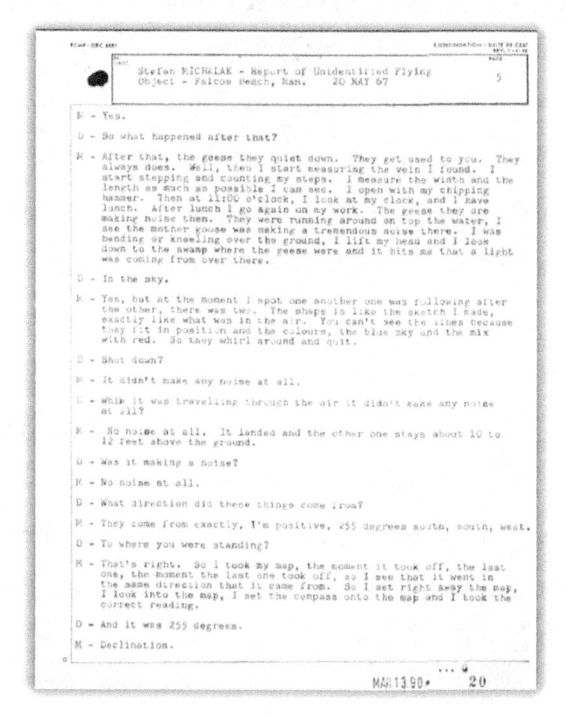

Chris Rutkowski's interview with Stephen Michalak
www.baclac.gc.ca/eng/discover/unusual/ufo/documents/interview-1967-05-24.pdf

RCMP Interview with Hotel Employees

On May 26, 1967, a report from Cpl. G.J. Davis of Winnipeg G.I. S. was forwarded to Constable L.A. Schmaltz of the Canadian Royal Mounted Police requesting that interviews be conducted with anyone at the Falcon Hotel who may have had contact with Stephen Michalak the evening prior to his alleged UFO sighting. The G.I.S. Geographic Information System is a database containing geographic data and descriptions of phenomena for a location with software that analyzes those data.

Mr. William Hastings, a bar tender stated he attended to the bar until 8:00 p.m. on May 19, but had not seen a man fitting his description. The manager of the bar and dining room took over at 8:00 p.m. and stated that Stephen was in the lounge, was served three bottles of beer, and left about 9:30 p.m. He then returned at 11:00 p.m. and had two more beers in the dining room. During that time he asked the manager whether many prospectors worked the area North of Falcon Lake Beach. The bartender thought Stephen was feeling the effects of the beer because he seemed so sure he would find something in the bush the next day.

Antje Poldervaart, the maid, stated that upon cleaning his room the next morning, she did not find any liquor bottles. Mrs. Martin Buseck, wife of the hotel owner, stated that Stephen approached her sometime in the early afternoon on May 20 in the parking lot. He was holding his jacket closed on his chest and inquired about a doctor. She told him there was no one available and wouldn't be until July 1. She advised him to seek out the RCMP if something was wrong. He left, but returned a short time later requesting to use a telephone in order to make a collect call to Winnipeg. She pointed out a telephone nearby.

All liquor purchases were checked at the Hotel and Government Liquor Store for May 20, but there were none.

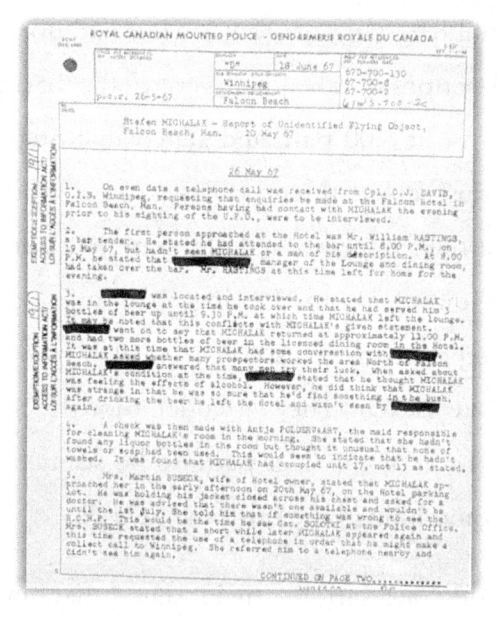

Witness Interviews by Cst. L. A. Schmaltz RCMP
May 26, 1967

Chosen

RCMP Interview with Stephen Michalak

On Tuesday morning, May 23, Inspector R. J. Ross the Assistant Criminal Investigation Branch Officer, C.I.B., instructed Cpl. G. J. Davis and Cst. Zacharias to visit Stephen Michalak at his residence in order to attempt to determine the authenticity of the report given by Stephen Michalak regarding his sighting of the two unidentified flying objects near Falcon Beach. Prior to speaking with Stephen, Cpl. Davis phoned Cst. Solotki who had encountered him on Saturday to get his version of the incident.

Upon arriving at 10:30 a.m. to the residence at 314 Lindsay Street, Winnipeg, Stephen his wife, and 19 year old son Mark were there. Also present at the time was J.B. Thompson from APRO, Aerial Phenomena Research Organization, which is a private organization investigating unidentified aerial phenomena. Thompson stayed awhile and left when they began a two hour interview with Stephen. He began relating the details of the event and his conversation with Cst. Solotki. He explained that he was hesitant to get close that day because he thought he was radioactive. Furthermore, he did not want to disclose the landing site because he had discovered a good nickel strike in the area and didn't want it to be common knowledge. When asked why he contacted the press, he said since he didn't get any satisfaction from speaking with the officer and feeling he needed medical attention, he phoned the Winnipeg Tribune from the hotel to see if they could do anything for him.

Stephen said upon arriving home, his son immediately drove him to Misericordia Health Center where he was examined and treated for first degree burns. In addition, he was treated by the family Dr. R. Douglas Oatray. Following their discussion, Cpl. Davis spoke with the doctor that afternoon who said besides the burns he couldn't find anything wrong with him mentally, but it appeared he had been through a traumatic event. The doctor then made arrangements with Dr. Gillies at the Winnipeg Cancer Research Clinic to determine if there was any radioactive material in the burn or the undershirt.

Stephen allowed them to examine the undershirt that he had been wearing the day of the incident. When they smelled it, they both agreed it smelled like burned electrical wiring or insulation. He had also been wearing a pair of yellow plastic gloves with a cloth insert and one of them had been burned on the fingertips. Before they had arrived, Mr. Thompson of APRO had taken that glove and they never recovered it from him.

Chosen

They asked Stephen to accompany them to the site, but he said he wasn't feeling well. Again on Tuesday, Wednesday, and Thursday they contacted him, but he was still very ill. In light of this, they obtained maps and aerial photographs from the Department of Mines and Natural Resources Surveys Branch.

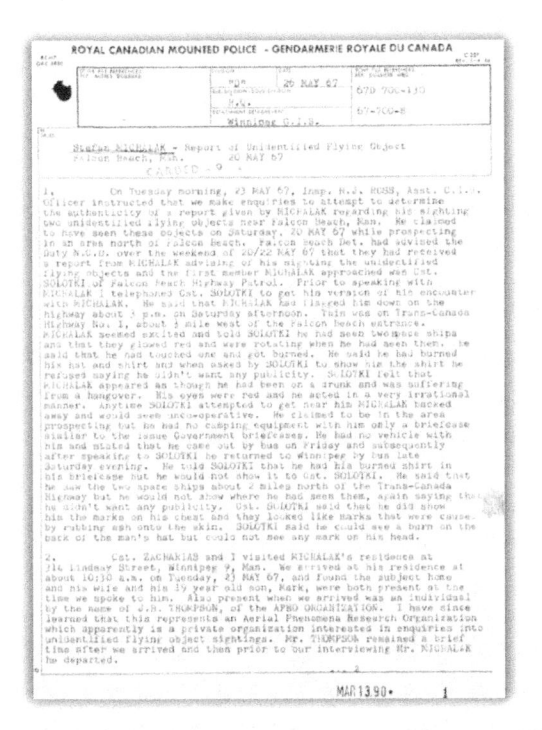

Interview of Stephen Michalak at his residence with Cpl. Davis and Cst. Zacharias - May 26, 1967
www.baclac.gc.ca/eng/discover/unusual/ufo/documents/1967-05-26.pdf

On May 30, they asked Stephen to draw a sketch of the terrain indicating the approximate area where he had seen the objects hoping this would enable them to locate the area without his being there.

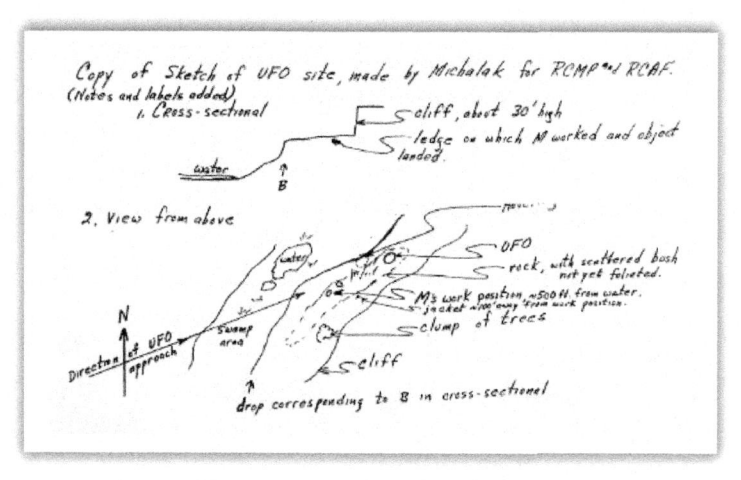

Map drawn by Stephen Michalak © RCMP and RCAF

Site Investigation

On May 31, Cpl. Davis and Cst. Anderson drove from Winnipeg to Falcon Lake where they met with seven members of the RCAF headed by Squadron Leader Bissky. At about 12:00 p.m. a Canadian Army helicopter piloted by Captain Bruce Muelander arrived from Rivers Air Station.

Cpl. Davis, Squadron Leader Bissky, and the pilot conducted a search by air attempting to find any indication of a landing site. Stephen had described a flat piece of rock approximately 300 feet long by 100 feet wide. Since such outcroppings of rock in the area were rare, they should be able to locate it. However, they were unable to locate any area that resembled what Stephen had sketched.

They landed on the Falcon Lake golf course and began to search on foot. The search continued until almost dark, but they were still unable to find the location. Upon further discussion, it was decided that continuing without him would be pointless. Cpl. Davis and Cst. Anderson drove back to Winnipeg attempting to convince Stephen to join them for at least one day. Although it was late evening, they drove directly to his residence. He agreed to search with them and arrangements were made to pick him up the following morning.

Cheryl Lynn Carter

© University of Ottawa Archives and Special Collections

Members of the investigation team included: Stewart Hunt of the Federal Heath Dept, Ottawa; Corporal C. J. Davis, RCMP; D. Thompson, Provincial Health Dept, Winnipeg; Stephen Michalak; Squadron Leader P. Bissky; Flight Lieutenant Smith, RCAF, Winnipeg; Constable J. Zacharias, RCMP, Winnipeg.

Searching for evidence of UFO landing
© Dept. of National Defense – Ottawa Archives

The Search with Stephen Michalak

Early in the morning on June 1, Cst. Anderson and Cpl. G.J. Davis picked up Stephen by police car. They made arrangements with the manager of the bar and dining room at Falcon Lake Hotel in order to confirm that Stephen was who he had seen. After talking with Stephen previously about what he did the night before the incident, there appeared to be conflicting information. The manager claimed he had first seen him about 8:00 p.m. However, the bus did not leave Winnipeg until 7:15 p.m. and it was a two hour trip which would get him there sometime between 9:15 and 9:30 p.m. He said he checked in and went to room 17 where he read his prospecting books until 11:00 p.m. He then went to the coffee shop for a hamburger and coffee where he spoke to a man about prospecting. He did not have any beers in fact he said he seldom drinks.

Cpl. Davis and the pilot took Stephen by helicopter to search for the area. However, the terrain looked markedly different from the air and he was unable to recognize any familiar land marks. In the afternoon, they went on foot and were able to locate the spot where somebody had left a saw and he had discarded a shopping bag. They continued to search all afternoon and into the evening covering about four miles of dense brush and outcroppings of rock, but he was unsure as to where he was going since as he said, nature changes quickly that time of year and the forest looked much different.

His explanation was that while he was prospecting he would follow quartz veins in the rocks and did not pay much attention to where he was walking. He would walk most of the day, but leave himself enough time to get out before dark. Taking a compass reading, he would head out in the direction he thought the highway was located. He did recall walking about 3,000 paces to the highway that day which he calculated to be about three miles.

The search continued to all the places that appeared similar to the map Stephen had drawn. However, they were unsuccessful in finding any evidence. They returned back to his home at about 10:00 p.m. The next morning, Cpl. Davis and Cst. Anderson returned to Falcon Lake to continue the search with members of the RCAF. By helicopter, they expanded the search from where they had previously searched. By mid afternoon without finding anything, they discontinued the search and returned back to Rivers.

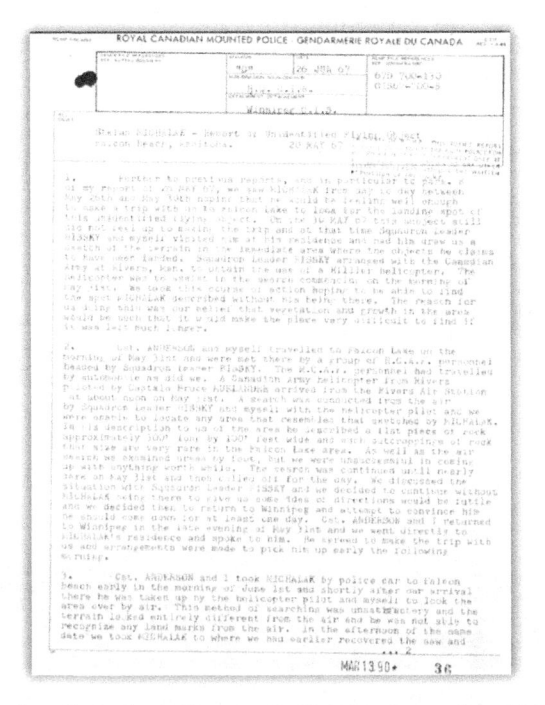

Report by Cpl. G. J. Davis, RCMP – June 26, 1967
www.bac-lac.gc.ca/eng/unusual/ufo/documents/1967-06-26.pdf

Stephen Returns to the Site

On June 30, Stephen contacted G.A. Hart who was an electronic engineer in Winnipeg. He too frequented the Falcon Lake area. Stephen asked if he might join him in search of the landing site and he agreed. They searched throughout the area looking for familiar rocks and examining chips he had made in the past.

Six hours later, they discovered the remains of his shirt, the tape measure, and the landing site. Strangely, the branches on the trees surrounding the landing area were withered and dead although all the other trees in the area were fine. After exploring the area a few minutes more, they were careful to mark their way so it would be easily found again.

The landing site © Stephen Michlak

Upon arriving back in Winnipeg, Stephen notified Squadron Leader Bissky and D. Thompson of the Health Department that they had located the landing site. On July 2, they traveled back to the area where they took additional samples and photos. Strangely enough after his return visit to the site, he began to feel ill again. He discovered several blisters near his throat and a mysterious rash appeared down the middle of his chest. He returned to Dr. Berger's office where he was treated and the rash disappeared a month later.

On August 10, 1967, a report from Cpl. G.J. Davis of Winnipeg G.I.S. was forwarded to the Royal Canadian Mounted Police concerning the landing site and soil sample. A.R. Corrigan of the Radiation Protection Division examined certain articles of Stephen's burned clothing, his steel tape, and a soil sample. They discovered that the tape and soil sample were highly radioactive containing .3 micro-curries of radium 226 a naturally occurring isotope and similarly found in nuclear waste.

Cheryl Lynn Carter

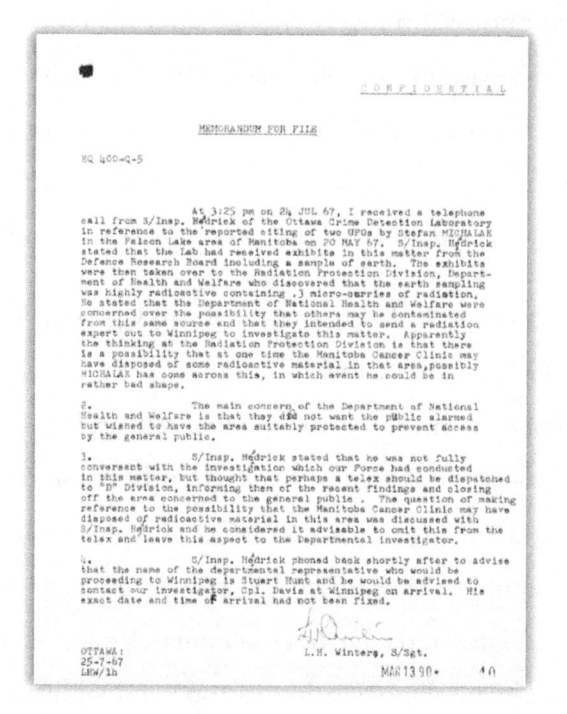

Report by Cpl. G.J. Davis forwarded to RCMP
August 10, 1967
www.baclac.gc.ca/eng/discover/unusual/ufo/documents/1967-08-10.pdf

Radiation Report

On September 13, 1967, a Memorandum #1107-4-6 from S. E. Hunt was sent to A. K. Das Gupta Head of Safety Assessment and Control. The subject: Determination of possible radiation hazards to the general public from the alleged landing site of an unidentified flying object near

Falcon Lake, Manitoba. A gamma ray spectral analysis of the three samples, the burnt shirt, steel tape, and soil sample, revealed activity levels of up to approximately 05 μCi of Ra 226. or 3.66.

RCMP Incident Report – analysis of samples

Still thinking that Stephen got his burns from work, on August 1, a visit was made to Inland Cement Company where he was employed as an Industrial Mechanic. They wanted to learn if the company used any radium sources in gauges and to inspect the company's Ohmart gauge, a nuclear density gauge. Radium is sometimes found in self-luminous paint that is used on dials and gauges. It could contain 1 microgram of radiation.

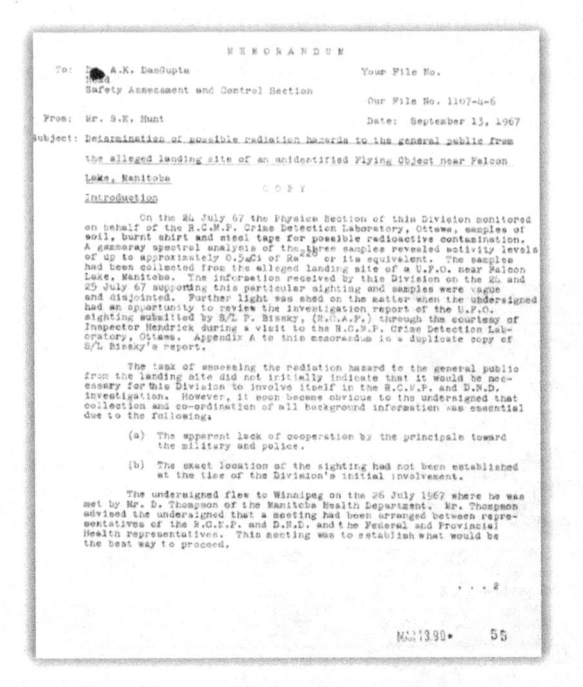

Safety Assessment Report to determine possible
radiation from an alleged UFO landing site
September 13, 1967
www.baclac.gc.ca/eng/discover/unusual/ufo/documents/1967-09-13.pdf

The area searched was located at approximately 49°43'+/- 1'N, 95°19'+/- 1'W within the forest. It contained dense vegetation, swamps, and rock outcroppings as much as 40 feet above the swamp level. At the landing site was a circle about 15 feet in diameter. The moss and vegetation no longer grew within a fifty foot radius. Soil samples tested to be highly radioactive at a count of 400 milliRoentgen. A year later, two radioactive twisted pieces of metal were found in a fissure at the site.

Piece of radioactive metal removed from a fissure
in the Precambrian Shield at the landing site.
© Stephen Michalak

Condon Committee

An investigation was conducted by Roy Craig of the Condon Committee, Boulder, Colorado in which Case #22 describes the interview and landing site investigation.

On September 13, Stuart E. Hunt of the Physics Section of the Safety Assessment and Control Section upon concluding the shirt and tape measure to be highly radioactive, sent a Memorandum with the Subject: Determination of possible radiation hazards to the general public from the alleged landing site of an unidentified flying object observed near Falcon Lake, Manitoba. They therefore considered restricting entry to that particular forest area.

An investigation was also conducted by Condon. A through survey of the landing site was conducted using a Tracerlab SU14, Admiral Radiac 5016, and a Civil Defense CDV 700 survey meter. It revealed that the perimeter of the landing circle and beyond was free of radiation. Only a small area measuring .5 x 8 inches on one side of the crack in the fissure was contaminated.

Two twisted pieces of metal were discovered about two inches below a layer of lichen in the rock fissure. Dr. Peter M. Millman of the National Research Council of

Canada sent them to R. J. Traill of the U.S. Nuclear Regulatory Commission. He interpreted the pieces to be thin sheets of silver that had been twisted and placed where they had contact with nearly pure quartz sand while still hot. They were covered with loosely adhering radioactive material consisting of crushed pitchblende ore and hematite. These are naturally occurring radioactive minerals that are typically in uraniferous deposits of the river area. He concluded that because of the thoroughness of all the earlier investigations of the site searching for radioactive material, it was highly unlikely that these would have missed had they been there all along.

Condon's conclusion states that Stephen Michalak's experience is questionable and does not show the existence of extraterrestrial crafts in our environment. They do not feel this case merits any further investigation.

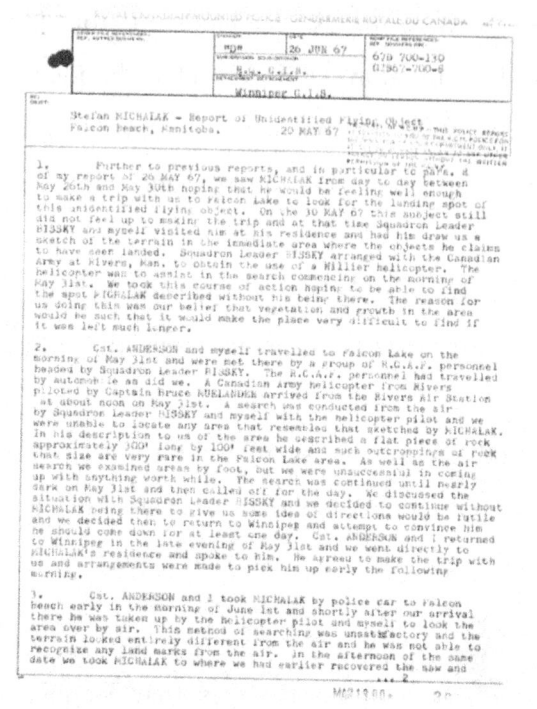

Condon Committee Report – September 13, 1967
Condon Committee/Report Investigation of Steven Michalak
Case - UFO Evidence

Contrary to Condon's conclusion, the case remains one of the most well known and well documented UFO cases involving close contact with the most detailed description of the object in Canadian History. It was investigated by the RCMP Royal Canadian Mounted Police, RCAF Royal Canadian Air Force, the DND Department of National

Defense, and Physicist Roy Craig of America's Condon Committee.

On September 21, five months after the initial encounter, he was outside working at the Inland Cement Company when he once again began to feel a burning sensation on his throat which he attributed to perhaps a bee sting. He went to the first aid room to get examined. By then, the pain was getting worse, his hands were swelling, and his face was purple. Upon removing his shirt, there were large red spots in the same area where the burns from the craft had been before. About fifteen minutes later, he became dizzy and found himself feeling faint. A fellow worker drove him to Misericordia Hospital for observation. Finally around 9:00 p.m. his symptoms began to subside. The doctor said it was caused by an allergy, but Stephen doubted it.

Canadian Press, November 6, 1967: According to Defense Minister Cadieux a report arising out of federal investigation into this sighting of an unidentified flying object at Falcon Lake, Manitobia, this year won't be made public. "It is not the intent of the Department of National Defense to make public the report of the alleged sighting." Nonetheless, Stefen thought that the public has a right to know if this craft came from Earth or another world. Furthermore, was it friendly or harmful?

Stephen Michalak attempted to leave the incident behind despite the continuous flash of reporter's cameras on his front lawn. He wrote a 39-page book about the event "My Encounter With the UFO" that he would distribute to friends. From time to time he worked on his claims at Falcon Lake. Whenever somebody asked him what he had seen that day, he always had the same reply, "I don't know. You tell me."

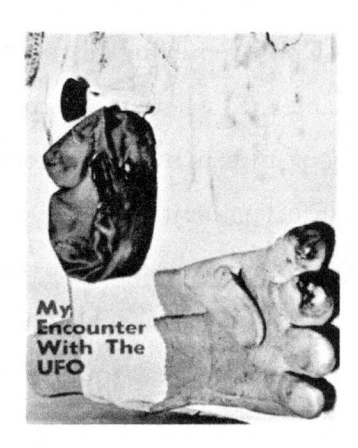

"My Encounter with the UFO" - Stephen Michalak - 1967
Translated from Polish to English by Paul Pihichyn
© University of Ottawa Archives and Special Collections

"When They Appeared: Falcon Lake 1967: Inside Story of a Close Encounter" Stan Michalak and Chris Rutkowski - 2019

Chapter 3
The Pascagoula Abduction

Calvin Parker first met Charlie Hickson in 1964 when his father Calvin and Charlie took the boys on fishing trips on the Pearl River. Many nights they all had dinner together with the family. Calvin Sr. and Charlie were good friends and as Calvin got older he got to know Charlie on a more personal level despite their age difference of 28 years. He remembered Charlie sometimes talking about his tour in Korea. Every time after a few minutes into a story, he would just stop talking about it. Nobody asked why.

One day Charlie came home from work and shared with them the unfortunate news that the company was shutting down. He began to search for another job and two weeks later he found one. Soon he would be moving because he had accepted the foreman position at a shipyard in Pascagoula, Mississippi and he would do his best to keep in touch.

In 1973, when Calvin was 19 years old, he began looking for a better job himself so he and his fiancé Waynette could purchase a house. His father suggested he contact Charlie because they were doing similar work. When he did,

Charlie was eager to help. The next morning, Calvin drove to Gautier, Mississippi, to meet up with him and his wife Blanche at the Collage Villa apartments.

Gautier is a small town west of Pascagoula and about a five minute drive to the shipyard. Charlie spent the weekend showing Calvin around as he looked for a place to stay. Without much success, they finally came back to Charlie's place. Since the apartment had three bedrooms, Charlie asked his wife if they might rent one room to Calvin. Blanche said yes and they agreed upon $50 a week. Calvin said he had to give notice at his present place of employment and would be back soon.

On the morning of Wednesday, October 3, Calvin drove back in his new 1973 Rambler Hornet and met Charlie at the gate of the F.B. Walker Shipyard. He escorted him to the office, where he filled out paperwork, and completed all the required safety training for the Shipfitter position. He would be part of a team responsible for building structural parts of ships such as plates, frames, and bulkheads and preparing them for welding.

Since they were living at the same residence, they would drive to work together in Calvin's new car. One night while passing by the Pascagoula River as they usually did,

Chosen

Charlie mentioned that he had caught a lot of fish there. On October, 11 at lunch time, he asked Calvin if he wanted to go fishing after work at his favorite spot on the Pascagoula River. Calvin had left his fishing gear back home and told Charlie he would have to stop and buy some. Charlie remarked that he had lots of fishing tackle and offered to let him use some. Calvin thought that was a generous gesture as most fishermen aren't inclined to share their gear.

After work, they went home, gathered the fishing gear, some shrimp bait, and Charlie told Blanche they would be back in a few hours. At 6:00 p.m. Calvin drove while Charlie shared the details about a spot on the Pascagoula River that was good for fishing. Ships unloading grain would sometimes spill some into the water and the fish would get under the elevator to feed on it.

Charlie Hickson and Calvin Parker

Before heading that way, he wanted to stop at a spot by the old Schaupeter Shipyard and try some fishing there. Upon pulling up, Calvin noticed "Posted" signs and was a bit concerned about breaking the law. Charlie assured him there was nothing to worry about because he fished there all the time. The shipyard had ceased operation quite awhile ago and the old road was now so littered with trash that they couldn't drive up to the water's edge. Charlie explained that when the water levels get high they wash a lot of trash and such from the road and nearby houses.

After parking about a hundred yards away, they walked through the tall marsh grass to the old pier on the west bank of the East Pascagoula River between the railroad and the high rise toll bridge on Highway 90. The old pier didn't appear structurally sound or safe to sit on. They found some old timber, sat down, cast out their lines, and waited. Charlie said this was a prime spot for Redfish and Speckled Trout and hopefully their bait would attract something. Although they both knew a trait of a good fisherman was patience, it soon began to grow dark and they weren't having much luck.

Calvin commented, "There's no fish here. Let's go to that old grain elevator that you were talking about." Charlie thought they should give it a few more minutes. Surely they would attract something … something.

Pier under the Highway 90 Bridge

Calvin noticed the reflection of blue hazy lights in the water. Thinking it was the police looking at his car he looked at Charlie and said, "Charlie, we're in trouble. You lied to me and we are fixin' to go to jail." Charlie was more focused on reeling in a fish only to discover it had just eaten his bait. He turned to get some more bait out of the cooler. As he did, a zipping sound caught his attention. It was almost like the sound of air escaping from a pipe. By now both men had turned around and as they stood up, they realized it wasn't the police. At this point, Calvin would have even welcomed them with open arms. He glanced at Charlie searching his face for some explanation, but he didn't have one.

About 25-30 yards away was the source of the bright blue light, a strange oval craft thirty feet long, eight feet high with a small dome-like structure on top, and something that resembled two windows. As it hovered about two feet off the ground, Charlie was convinced it wasn't any known aircraft because there was no engine sound or wings. Instantly, he began weighing his options as to which way to run, but there was no time for that.

"What do they want?" Charlie shouted. As if to answer his question, a hatch opened and three creatures floated from the craft and moved towards them. They were about five feet tall with the head connected directly to the shoulders. There was a point where the nose would be and similar points on each side of the head where ears would be. Directly under the center point was a slit resembling a mouth. The bodies were wrinkled grey similar to elephant skin, with long arms, hands that resembled claws, and legs that remained together.

Chosen

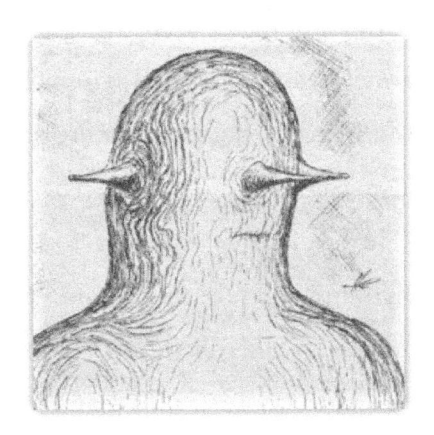

© Drawings by Jason Gleaves courtesy Flying Disk Press

Two creatures grabbed hold of Charlie's arms and he immediately felt a sharp pain in his left shoulder. The other one grabbed Calvin and the two men unable to resist floated through the air and into the craft.

Charlie's first thoughts were of reading accounts of people disappearing. Was it going to happen to them? Once inside, there was a blinding light, they were separated, and he was taken down a hallway to a room. The creature floated him to a table. He felt like he was at a forty-five angle, but couldn't feel anything solid beneath him. Perhaps he was feeling nothing at all. Charlie called out, "Please don't take me away," although he could not hear his own voice.

The creature left the room and a smaller being appeared. It was grey, five feet tall, small head, thin face, with big dark eyes. This one seemed some-what human while the others were more mechanical. A device came down from the ceiling that looked like a big eye. There was something attached to it that scanned his body making a clicking sound as if it was taking pictures. After the examination, the beings had moved away, but Charlie still was unable to move. "Where is Calvin?" he asked, but he still could not hear his voice.

After what seemed like forever, the creatures returned. They took the men to an opening in the ship and they felt themselves floating back down the blue light and returning to the bank of the river. Charlie was unharmed, but when he looked over at Calvin he was concerned because Calvin appeared to be going into the state of shock. Before he could reach him, there was a zipping sound, a blue flashing light, and the craft was instantly gone. For some reason a thought crossed his mind, "We are peaceful. We meant you no harm."

As he reached Calvin, he began to shake him. Thinking the creatures still had control over him, Calvin flinched and cried out, "Please don't!" Charlie shook him a little harder, he finally relaxed, and fell to the ground. Calvin looked around still wondering where the beings were and what they were going to do to them. "The craft is gone. You need to relax," Charlie said as he tried to bring him back to reality although at the moment he wasn't quite sure what reality was himself.

His mind flashed backed to another place; a place far away: 1952, ten thousand miles away in North Korea north of the 30th Parallel. His unit had been called to help stop an attack where the north Koreans and Chinese had broken the lines of the First Capital Division of the South Korean Army. Was he scared? Yes, but tonight was different. Something from another place, another world, something that is not supposed to exist appeared and they were chosen. Tonight he experienced fear like he had never felt before.

Calvin slowly began to respond saying that it seemed as if he died and came back to life. Charlie tried to reassure him that everything was okay, even though he was having a difficult time believing that himself.

"Calvin, we have got to forget about this and not tell anyone."

"I might not tell anyone," Calvin replied, "but I won't ever forget it."

For a few minutes they sat down on the log in silence neither of them knowing what to say. Charlie began wondering if he could live the rest of his life without telling anyone.

Calvin looked over at Charlie and asked, "Shouldn't we tell someone? What if those things come back?"

They discussed the probability for a few minutes. Charlie felt that they needed to inform the military and Calvin agreed. Eager to get out of there, they quickly gathered the fishing gear and made their way through the tall grass and back to the car. Upon reaching the car, they noticed one of the windows was completely shattered. The glass was still in the frame, but when the door was opened it all fell out.

Calvin's thoughts quickly went from otherworldly things to his car of which he had only made one payment.

During the drive back, they searched for a pay phone. Charlie located one, dropped in a dime, and called Keesler Air Force Base in Biloxi. He asked to speak to someone in authority concerning the mysterious craft. Before he could offer any additional details, they quickly stopped him, saying since the end of Project Blue Book they no longer handled UFO reports, and he should contact the sheriff.

Frustrated, Charlie picked up the phone once more and called the Jackson County Sheriff's Department. His thought was that after he explained what had happened they would contact the proper authorities. He just wasn't sure who that might be since the Air Force had turned him away. However, after he briefly described what happened, he felt like the deputy thought it was all a hoax. He told them to come right over and they could talk. Determined to prove just how real it was, they headed over to the office.

Cheryl Lynn Carter

Jackson County Sheriff Interview

When they arrived at the Jackson County Sheriff's Department, Charlie insisted they not notify the media. Sheriff Fred Diamond assured them that whatever was said in the office would not go any further. The men were put into separate rooms and questioned by Sheriff Fred Diamond. They had no idea they were secretly being recorded because it was legal at the time. Their accounts were identical making the sheriff believe they had indeed experienced a terrifying event. Then they were both left alone in a room in order to see if their story would change. They never wavered from their original story.

Sheriff Fred Diamond

Chosen

Secret Taped Conversation

The following is part of the 30 minute taped conversation of the two men thinking they were alone:

Calvin: "Do you reckon there is anything that the U.S. would have that looked like that?"

Charlie: "No, no it just couldn't be. Not what we seen though."

Calvin: "What do you think they were?"

Charlie: "All I remember is a blur kinda look on their face. I distinctly remember their hands. Their face was just like a ghost. Just like you look through that wall right there and see a ghost or something come through. I don't know if I was scared or what; it was just blurred."

Calvin: "You hear about something like that, but you can't believe it."

Charlie: "This ain't going to be the only time. It's going to happen again. Until they …"

Calvin: "It scared the hell out of me tonight. I came damn near dying. Right now, I can't take it."

Charlie: "I know it's something you can't get over in a life time. Nobody's going to believe it. That's the trouble. I thought I'd been through enough hell on this Earth and now I have to go through something like this. But they could have harmed us, son. They had us. They could have done anything to us."

Calvin: "I wonder why they picked us up."

Charlie: "I don't know. I'm telling you, man. I couldn't take much more of that."

Calvin: "I got to get home to bed … see a doctor or something. I can't stand it. I'm about to go all to pieces."

Charlie: "I'll tell you, when they get through with us, I'll get you something to settle you down so you can get some damn sleep."

Calvin: "I can't sleep now. I'm just damn near crazy."

Charlie: "Damn when they brought you out of that thing … when they brought me out … Well, I like to never in the hell got you straightened out, man."

Calvin: "I don't know. All I remember was my eyes. They just froze up like that. I couldn't move 'em."

Charlie: "They didn't do me that way though."

Calvin: "I passed out. That's the first time I ever passed out in my life … I don't care if they should believe it or not, but I do know better."

Charlie: "They had better wake up and start believing."

Calvin: "I can't figure out how the damn thing opened. Did you see how that door come right open in front of us all of a sudden?"

Charlie: "I don't know how it opened, son. I don't know. I've never seen nothing like that before in my life. You can't make people believe."

Calvin: "I can't figure out the damn door. You see how that door comes around on our side of the ship? I didn't see no door swing open. All I know is I looked around, then the damn blue lights, and them sons-a-bitches just walked out and came down."

Charlie: "They're going to believe it one of these days. It might be too late. I knew all along there were people from other worlds up there. I knew all along. I never thought it would happen to me."

Cheryl Lynn Carter

The Day After

Friday morning, Calvin awoke, gathered everything he was wearing the night before, and put it into a garbage bag. Charlie noticed bleeding from what appeared to be a small puncture wound on his upper left arm in the exact area where the strange creature had grabbed him. He wiped it with his handkerchief and didn't think too much about it. All they wanted to do was leave yesterday behind them. When they got into the car, Calvin tired to start it, but it was running rough. He discovered three of the spark plugs were bad; plugs on a car only a month old.

Charlie did his best to focus at work as he got his crew ready for the day. His mind began to wander back to last night, but he quickly managed to gain control of his thoughts again. Calvin on the other hand was not as fortunate. Everyone could see something was wrong with him. Before Charlie was able to take him aside and see if he could help, he was called to the phone. It was a reporter from Jackson, Mississippi asking about what happened. Thinking it was quite odd he merely said no comment. However, that was only the beginning. The phones at the shipyard continued to ring with people asking to speak to Charlie and Calvin. It was obvious that the sheriff had not kept his word.

Chosen

Charlie called the Sheriff's Office and Sheriff Fred Diamond answered. He quickly denied having any knowledge of who leaked the story.

"Charlie, I don't know how it leaked out of this office, but anyway we can't keep a story like this from the world. Can you and Calvin come in?"

Furious, Charlie slammed down the phone and uttered a few swear words. Jim Flynt and Danny Davis who were foremen had heard part of the conversation with the Sheriff's Office. Of course, now he needed to explain without giving up too much of the story. No sooner had Charlie offered an explanation when they were called into the General Manager's office.

Oliver Bryant the GM and Johnny Walker the owner asked them to sit down and explain what had happened last night. As Charlie and Calvin related their story to them, they were very understanding. Charlie also stated that the Sheriff wanted them to return to his office. After taking it all in, Johnny Walker suggested they seek legal counsel with Joe Colingo the Shipyard's attorney. He would also deal with any media requests. The legal contract only lasted a week before Charlie cancelled it because he could see Joe Colingo was only interested in financial gain.

Upon arriving at the Sheriff's Office, they were confronted by a swarm of reporters so they were safely escorted to the back entrance. From there they went directly to Sheriff Diamond's office and the first thing Joe Colingo did was ask if they could administer a polygraph test. The sheriff remarked that they did not have such equipment and it would be pointless because they already had that secret tape recording from last night. Upon hearing that, Charlie glared at Sheriff Diamond. Joe Colingo insisted that it was indeed important, but nobody appeared interested in the idea.

While everyone was debating about the polygraph test, Charlie suddenly realized something. What if they had come in contact with radiation last night? If they were contaminated, were they putting everyone that they had recent contact with in danger? He threw his hands up and voiced his concern as to why everyone was debating the polygraph when what they actually needed was a radiation test. Detective Tom Huntley and Joe Colingo were in agreement. They ushered them to a car at the back entrance and rushed them to the Singing River Hospital to be tested. However, upon arriving at the hospital, the physician informed them the hospital was not able to perform such a test.

Detective Huntley immediately called Keesler Air Force Base that agreed to conduct the test. Charlie and Calvin didn't say much on the way because they were nervous about the outcome. It was thirty-five miles to the base and it felt like forever before their car pulled up to the gates where the M.P.'s were waiting. Once inside the base, they were given directions to the area where the Radiation Team was waiting. Charlie and Calvin began to get even more nervous when the personnel were all wearing protective clothing. What was going to happen if they were indeed exposed to radiation? Fortunately, the test proved negative, but there was something odd in their blood.

Kessler Field UFO Interrogation

After the radiation test, they were escorted down the hall to a door with dark windows that they couldn't see through. They sat in the room a few minutes before six military men and a man in a black suit came in.

Among those present were Lt. Col. Barrington, Security Police; Cpt. Hoban and MSgt. Russell, Security Police; Lt. Col. Gibson, Associate Administrator; T.E.

Huntley, Detective Jackson County Sheriff's; and Joe Colingo, Attorney.

The Man in Black asked all the questions and once again Charlie and Calvin related their story. Afterwards, they were handed a paper of what was said to contain the minutes of the meeting; a paper that was blank. They were told to just sign it and an official copy would be mailed to them. As for what the contents of the report included, they would never know because they never received a copy.

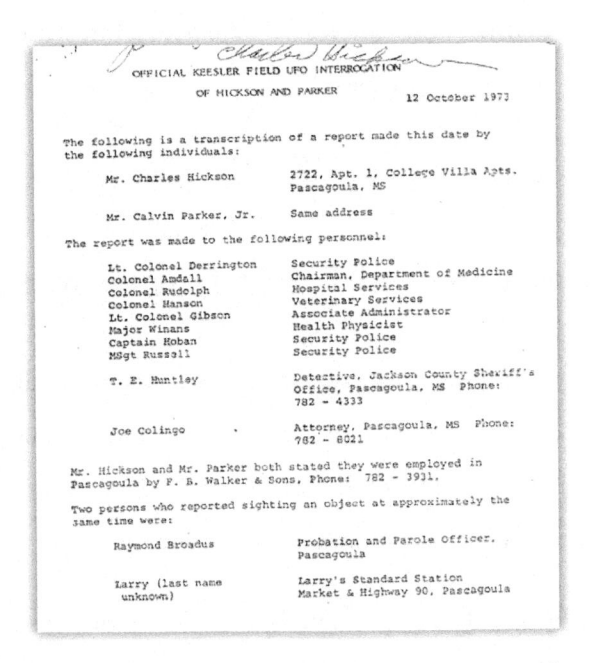

```
       Charles Hickson
OFFICIAL KEESLER FIELD UFO INTERROGATION
       OF HICKSON AND PARKER          12 October 1973

The following is a transcription of a report made this date by
the following individuals:

    Mr. Charles Hickson      2722, Apt. 1, College Villa Apts.
                             Pascagoula, MS

    Mr. Calvin Parker, Jr.   Same address

The report was made to the following personnel:

    Lt. Colonel Derrington   Security Police
    Colonel Amdall           Chairman, Department of Medicine
    Colonel Rudolph          Hospital Services
    Colonel Manson           Veterinary Services
    Lt. Colonel Gibson       Associate Administrator
    Major Winans             Health Physicist
    Captain Hoban            Security Police
    MSgt Russell             Security Police

    T. E. Huntley            Detective, Jackson County Sheriff's
                             Office, Pascagoula, MS  Phone:
                             782 - 4333

    Joe Colingo              Attorney, Pascagoula, MS  Phone:
                             782 - 8021

Mr. Hickson and Mr. Parker both stated they were employed in
Pascagoula by F. B. Walker & Sons, Phone: 782 - 3931.

Two persons who reported sighting an object at approximately the
same time were:

    Raymond Broadus          Probation and Parole Officer,
                             Pascagoula

    Larry (last name         Larry's Standard Station
    unknown)                 Market & Highway 90, Pascagoula
```

Title page of the Kessler Field UFO Interrogation
October 12, 1973

Chosen

Dr. J. Allen Hynek

On Saturday, Charlie and Calvin went back to the shipyard and the office of Johnny Walker. There they would meet with Dr. James Harder, professor at the University of California who was associated with APRO the Aerial Phenomena Research Organization and Dr. J. Allen Hynek, professor of Astronomy at Northwestern University in Illinois who worked with Project Blue Book. As they began their story, Dr. Harder would interrupt to ask questions; questions that they sometimes could not answer. He then told them that Dr. Hynek would be arriving at 2:00 p.m. and that they would like to speak to them under a hypnotic state. Charlie wasn't must interested in that idea, but at 2:00 they could all discuss the possibility.

In the meanwhile, Charlie and Calvin went back home for lunch. It was probably the best meal they had since Thursday night. Then they headed back to Johnny Walker's office to meet Dr. Hynek. Just as in the morning with Dr. Harder when they began to relate their story, Dr. Hynek interrupted with more questions. And once again, there were questions they could not answer. Dr. Harder and Dr. Hynek decided that it would be beneficial to do hypnosis and began to explain the process. Hypnotic regression allows a person to retrieve information in our mind which has been stored at an unconscious level.

Dr. James Harder and Dr. J. Allen Hynek

Charlie Hickson Regression

John Kraus and Charlie Hickson

Chosen

John Kraus, founder and director of the Kraus Hypnosis Centre in Detroit, Michigan conducted the sessions. Present were Charlie, John Kraus, and Curtis Watkins an artist who sketched Charlie's descriptions. The regression lasted thirty minutes. The following is part of Charlie's session.

Kraus: "What's happening now?"

Charlie: "Calvin! Calvin! Did you hear that? Oh my God! What is it? It's got some blue lights on it. It's … it's not touching the ground."

Kraus: "Look at it close. Don't be afraid."

Charlie: "Something is opening in that thing. That light is so bright, so bright. It's pretty big."

Kraus: "What's pretty big?"

Charlie: "Well, that, that out there! It looks … I don't know what the hell it looks like. It's got something on top of it too. There's someone comin' through the doorway. I can't tell what it is yet."

Kraus: "Watch it, watch it. Don't be afraid, just watch it."

Charlie: "Oh my God! What am I gonna do? I can't move. I can't run … nothing. They're comin' out. What is it? Calvin!

What is it? They're getting closer! I can't move! There's three of 'em. I can see 'em better now. Whatever it is, they're moving toward us. I can't tell yet, they're not on the ground. I don't know … something that looks like that! They don't look like anything I've ever seen."

Kraus: "Don't be afraid now Charlie."

Charlie: "They're gonna take hold of me. That light! They're getting on me! Something got my left shoulder. I got a sharp pain there. Oh Lord! They got Calvin too."

After the session, Charlie received a phone call from his son saying he needed to come home because his wife was really upset. It would appear reporters were now calling the house. They quickly said their good-byes and Charlie and Calvin crossed the West River Bridge heading back home to Gautier.

They didn't talk on the way except for when Calvin said, "Charlie, I wished they would have killed me. I can't take much more of this."

Witnesses

On the opposite side of the river, Maria and Vernon Jerry Blair were sitting in their 1969 maroon Pontiac Grand Am in the parking lot of Graham's Seafood where Jerry was a Captain of one of Graham's ships. He was preparing to leave on a boat to work off shore.

They had just found out the captain coming from Orange Beach was going to be late because there had been bad weather. It was getting dark and Jerry decided to take a nap since he would be up all night. Their car was facing the water in such a manner that they had a view of the east bank of the Pascagoula River. Charlie and Calvin were fishing on the west bank so the Blairs were not able to see them.

Maria looked up at the sky and observed what she thought was a plane because it had bright blue and green flashing lights. However as she watched, the object moved silently and the flight pattern and intermittent hovering were not indicative of a helicopter or plane. For thirty-five minutes she watched as the object flew towards the gulf, came back, and circled above the west bank of the Pascagoula River by the bridge.

Jerry woke up and told her to walk down the pier with him so he could put his belongings into the boat. It was now dark as they began to walk down the hill with Jerry leading the way. Maria heard a splashing sound, looked down to see something come out of the water and go back down. She thought it was a person wearing something like a grey diver's suit, but Jerry dismissed it as being a porpoise. She stopped, watched, and waited thinking they had to eventually come back up for air, but the water stopped rippling.

By this time, Jerry was far ahead of her so she hurried to catch up. He boarded the boat, reiterated that there was nobody in the water, and said good night. Nonetheless, since it was now 11:30 p.m. and she was walking down the pier alone, she ran back to the car.

Years later, Jerry spoke about what he had actually seen that night. For years he had kept quiet fearing people would consider him crazy, but he did indeed see everything Maria saw and more. At the time in his mind, he could not comprehend it was real. He saw the humanoid figure in the water that made the splashing sound: it wasn't a porpoise like he told Maria. He saw the blue light come down, the grey beings floating in the air away from them towards the other side of the river, and into some sort of ship before it shot off into the sky.

Chosen

Maria and Vernon Blair

Larry Booth, a WWII Air Corps veteran, was the proprietor of Larry's Standard Station located at Market Street and Highway 90. At 9:00 p.m. he went to make sure his front door was locked before going to bed. He turned off the lights and reached over to turn off the outside light. When he happened to look through the glass on the door, he observed a huge object in the sky. It hovered about eight feet above the telephone pole. There were red lights all around it that were turning in a clock-wise motion. There were neither wings nor sound. He knew it wasn't a helicopter because flying this low the vibration would have jarred everyone in the house.

Suddenly, the object began to slowly move directly over the pine tree. As it moved more in the distance he could see it was dome-shaped with a small dome on top. He really didn't think more about it because he knew Kessler and Pensacola were always running some kind of experiment. That was until the following morning when he turned on the news and heard about what had happened to the two men. He immediately phoned Kessler Air Force Base and reported his sighting.

Larry Booth

Chosen

Navy Petty Officer Mike Cataldo, Ted Peralta, and Mack Hanna had just left the Ingalls Shipyard. It was not yet dusk when they got into Peralta's Volkswagen and traveled down Highway 90 going west towards Buloxi. They looked up to see a very strange object in the horizon going from the northeast across Highway 90. At first they thought it was a shooting star. They pulled off the road and watched as it came down into a marshy, tree lined area, and hovered for about a minute. The object, about a half mile away, was light grey, similar in shape to a sailor hat, as big as an American airliner., and had blinking lights on the top. Then it shot away at a high rate of speed and was gone.

Cataldo parted company with the others and got into his own vehicle. Darkness was now setting in as he was in enroute to Ocean Springs. He observed the same object a second time at a distance away, watched it for about forty-five seconds, and it shot off in the same direction as before.

The following day, the three men returned to the shipyard and began talking about what they had seen the previous night. As a member of the pre-commissioning crew of the USS Tunney that was under construction at Ingalls, Cataldo felt that he needed to make a statement so he approached Executive Commander Lieutenant Heath and issued a verbal report of the sighting, but to his knowledge, no written report was ever made. In fact, no one ever asked him about it again.

On Sunday morning, he saw the headline in the morning paper about two men that had been taken aboard a flying saucer. He placed a call to a Public Relations Officer at Kessler Air Force Base, but again nothing resulted from his report.

Budd Hopkins Regression - Calvin

On March 14, 1993, Calvin was given the opportunity to have Budd Hopkins, New York Times best-selling author of UFO abduction phenomena, conduct a regressive hypnosis session with him.

Calvin: "Sounds like raining dripping; just a steady drip, drip, drip. I think it's my blood ... my right hand. I'm bleeding on the outside of my hand. She's cut it. And I don't remember what it is she put in my right hand ... Oh, I see now, black and it resembles a needle. And there's a serious cut and now she's cutting into my right hand right on the outside. And then, it's like a miracle, it just quit bleeding and it's healed. But there's some object, definitely still there, it's in my hand."

Hopkins: "There's an object inside your hand?"

Calvin: "Yes, she put it there."

Hopkins: "Look around and you might see something similar that looks like writing, some kind of funny writing … on the table or on the wall, or anything."

Calvin: "No writing … I'm looking around. I'm looking at the ceiling, I'm looking at the floor, and I'm looking around for a door to get out. I know I came through a door. I see me in a mirror, but I'm not here by myself. I have the strange feeling that I'm being watched. Electricity is bouncing off the walls … little balls of electricity just bouncing and bouncing. I remember dodging them from one side to the other."

Hopkins: "What did she say to you?"

Calvin: "She just talked to me, but she wasn't moving her mouth. She's pulling thoughts out of my head, everything that I know and she's pulling thoughts out, and then she tells me 'You're not gonna be any danger to us.' … I remember thinking who is us? She said, 'You will no longer be a threat.' I didn't know I was a threat to start with, but she can bet that I will be a threat from now on. She's evil, really evil. I'm able to see things that I've never seen before."

Hopkins: "What are you seeing?"

"My soul is leaving me body!"

Calvin: "Another light shines on me and it's beautiful and she's afraid of this light. She's really afraid of this light. She's turning her head now, she's getting back into the corner, and trying to get at the door where this light's shining on me. And through this light I can see things that I've never known. It's like sitting back and watching a movie and being able to see into the future through this light."

Hopkins: "What are some of the things you see?"

Calvin: "I feel a real warm sensation, the best feeling I ever had in my life. Thank God I'm finally dead; I'm dead. And my soul is leaving my body. She's actually killed me; my soul's leaving my body. In this light, this strong light, I'm glad it's all over now. I'll finally get some peace. And then I see angels, nothing like I've ever seen before. Oh, oh, I'm being pulled back down; I'm being pulled back into my body. I don't wanna go back into my body. I just want to leave. I want to go into this light. It just felt so good. Let me go back into this light. Don't send me back. Lord, please take me, take me. Let me come to you. I don't want to go back, but I have to go back ... I have to go back. I must go back. I must go back to my body now, I must."

"I'm back in my body. I'm in a standing position. It's not right to hate your fellow man, but I hate what's going on. It's like what's she afraid of? And I see destruction. I see the world being changed for what it's like. I see them possessing bodies, taking them over. Again, I have a power to fight it. Again I can see through her now and the light's gone. I'm at total peace with myself ... She turned around and looked. She won't come around now. She's backing away, backing through the door, and she's gone. She's out of sight ... I feel at peace now. I feel it's over now.

And they escort me out the door, the same one that brought me in, and I'm back into this little ball, and I'm being carried back out. In see Charlie still standing on the pier. I'm still in the little ball. I see Charlie on the pier and he's standing there as though he's paralyzed. I'm thinking what did they do to him? And then they put me down, and I'm facing the water, and my arms are stretched out over the water and Charlie runs to me and says are you ok. And Charlie's shaking me; he's shaking me like I've never been shaken before. I could feel Charlie shaking me, but I can't react. Charlie's wanting to talk. He's talking to me and I don't want to talk no more."

Cheryl Lynn Carter

Budd Hopkins and Kathleen Marden

Kathleen Marden Regression - Calvin

Kathleen Marden is the Director of MUFON's UFO Experiencer Research Team, on the Board of Directors of Dr. Edgar Mitchell Foundation for Extraterrestrial and Extraordinary Encounters, Practitioner of QHHT Quantum Healing Hypnosis, and niece of Betty and Barney Hill. The following is part of a session she conducted with Calvin on September 14, 2019:

Kathleen: "Okay, and then what happened?"

Calvin: "I noticed some lights across the water, there were blue lights reflecting and I figured we were going to jail. So, I stood up and turned around and I guess Charlie noticed them at the same time I did. And he turned around too and all of a sudden there was a bright light that come on us, way bright, almost blinding."

Kathleen: "Are you looking at it? Is Charlie looking at it?"

Calvin: "I'm looking at it, towards it. He is now, and I noticed Charlie's face has got a serious look on it. That's when he kinda backed up just a step and I noticed it too, something was coming towards us … It was, you can make three figures out. It looked like they were just flying over the top of the grass, effortlessly coming towards us."

Kathleen: So, what thoughts passed through your mind?"

Calvin: "To run like hell, but there was nowhere to go."

After being taken aboard the craft …

Kathleen: "What did it look like?"

Calvin: "It looked like a woman. Just a regular person coming towards me … This lady had brown eyes. She was thin. Had a nose, eyes, mouth, and her skin was pale."

Kathleen: "Have you seen this woman before?"

Calvin: "Yes, two times … when I was twelve.'

Kathleen: "What are you thinking now? What thoughts come to you?"

Calvin: "A bad day to come fishing."

Kathleen: "Was she giving you any message?"

Calvin: "My whole life passed in front of me. And yes, she was, tried to get me all in the future. But there was no future at the end of the message."

Kathleen: "What were you seeing in that message all in the future?"

Calvin: "I saw a mushroom, with bright lights and the people's faces melting off."

Kathleen: "Did you feel like you were taken into the future or into the past?"

Calvin: "It was grim, the future … people starving and dying."

Kathleen: "Did she tell you that's the future of Earth or the future or past of where she came from?"

Calvin: "She never said."

Kathleen: "Now leave that scene and go back to the first time you ever saw that lady. The first time you ever remember seeing that lady."

Calvin: "The first time I seen her we were fishing. We went to Pearl River with some friends, and we were fishing, and she was in the woods. And she tried to get me to come over and I didn't see her face or nothing real good then, but she motioned me to come there. And a friend of ours was calling his kids and all, and we went over, so I didn't go there."

Kathleen: "When you were fishing on the Pearl River who was with you?"

Calvin: "My father, my brother, Charlie Hickson, Sheila Hickson, and Eddie Hickson."

Kathleen: "Okay, how old were you that day?"

Calvin: "I'd be 12-13 years old."

Kathleen: "And what happened next? You saw her and what happened next?"

Calvin: "Charlie was calling me. And when he called my name she ran off into the woods and I didn't see her any more that night."

Kathleen: "How close was she to you when you saw her?"

Calvin: "She was probably ten feet."

Kathleen: "Was there anything unusual about this girl that wanted you to walk into the woods?"

Calvin: "Besides from being in the middle of nowhere in the woods by herself, now that was unusual. But other than that, no."

"It's foolish to look up in the sky, see all these stars, and think that we're the only life."

Life was never the same after that night. Charlie returned to work at the shipyard and family life although it was always on his mind. He continued to give interviews and later wrote a book "UFO Contact at Pascogoula."

Calvin found it difficult to deal with the constant reporters at the shipyard gates so he moved back home to Laurel where he found new employment with Exarter Drilling working in the oil field. He married Waynette and changed his name. She finally encouraged him to write two books "Pascagoula - The Closest Encounter: My Story" and "Pascagoula - The Story Continues: New Evidence and Witnesses."

Chosen

In September 2019, Pascagoula Mayor Dane Maxwell commemorated a historical marker in honor of their story. The dedication took place next to the Lighthouse Park boat launches.

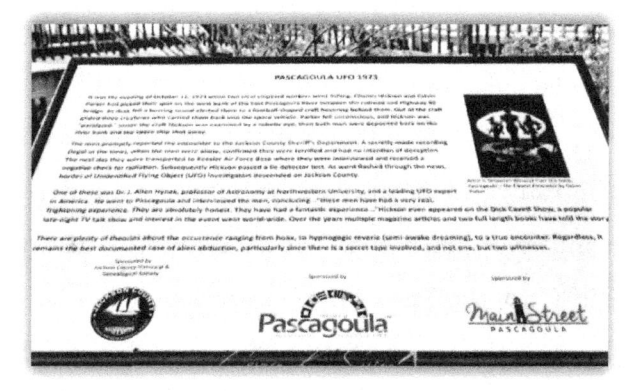

Historical Marker

"UFO Contact at Pascagoula" Charles Hickson and William Mendez - 2017

"Pascagoula: The Closest Encounter: My Story" Calvin Parker - 2018

"Pascagoula: The Story Continues: New Evidence and Witnesses" Calvin Parker – 2019

University of Ottawa Library Network – Archives and Special Collections, Ontario, Canada

Chapter 4
Rendlesham Forest

Situated on the east coast in the county of Suffolk, England is 5.8 square mile woodland comprised of tall Corsican pines known as Rendlesham Forest. It sits adjacent to the Royal Air Force twin bases of Bentwaters and Woodbridge. Bentwaters, constructed in 1942, was named after two Bentwaters cottages that once stood on the site of the main runway and was first operated by the RAF Bomber Command. Woodbridge, constructed in 1943, was named for the nearby town of Woodbridge. In September of 1951, the bases became the home of the 81st Tactical Fighter Wing.

Operated by the United States Air Force, they provided a vital part of NATO's defense against Communist threats. Woodbridge was chosen as a site to assist distressed aircraft to land on return flights from raids in Germany because it was a nearly fog free, unobstructed approach from both the west and east. During the Cold War, there was a secret joint project between the United States and United Kingdom known as Project Emily. This agreement was to coordinate the strike plans of the U.S. and U.K. bomber forces and to store U.S. nuclear weapons in bunkers on RAF airfields. PGM-17 Thor, named after the Norse god of

Thunder, was the first intermediate-range ballistic missile with a thermonuclear warhead. There were a number of nuclear weapons at Bentwaters stored in fortified underground bunkers known as "Hot Row."

Security and Law Enforcement operated as separate entities and were both vital components to maintaining the integrity of the bases. Staff Sergeant James W. Penniston age 25, the Security Supervisor holding top secret U.S. and NATO security clearances, had been with the Air Force since 1973 and was stationed at RAF Bentwaters since June 1980. His duties entailed ensuring the base was protected from any terrorist activity and anything else that might jeopardize both the safety and operational status of equipment.

SSgt. James Penniston's senior Law Enforcement counterpart at RAF Woodbridge was Staff Sergeant Bud Steffans who had been stationed there approximately three months.

Airman First Class John Frederick Burroughs age 20 had been with the Air Force since March 1979. He had been stationed at RAF Bentwaters for seventeen months where he was assigned to the Law Enforcement Squadron and was recently assigned to RAF Woodbridge.

At 6:00 p.m. on December 25, 1980, SSgt. James Penniston was about to begin the last midnight shift of his six day tour before a well deserved three day rest. He reported for duty at RAF Bentwaters as did the twelve men of his squad. One of the men was newly assigned Airman First Class Edward N. Cabansag. Guard Mount was conducted consisting of roll call, weapons and equipment inspection, and announcements. Their assignment was to report to RAF Woodbridge for their shift as Security Eight.

As the Base Security Supervisor of RAF Woodbridge, during his shift he was responsible for any security situation that might occur on the base. In addition at his discretion, he could utilize Law Enforcement patrols to work in conjunction with Security as reinforcement.

SSgt. James Penniston began conducting the base perimeter check including perimeter lighting and security check of the buildings. Since it was Christmas, it was down time for any aircraft maintenance making the base fairly quiet. He recorded notes that he would submit to Master Sergeant Preston who was his reporting official. A few hours later after completing his check, he met up with Security Six and Sergeant McCulley where they decided to meet at the chow hall at 11:50 p.m. for dinner.

Chosen

At 11:00 p.m. A1C John Burroughs of Law Enforcement Flight C arrived and began his routine patrol around the base perimeter in his patrol car. SSgt. Bud Steffens, his senior partner and superior, arrived shortly after and radioed him suggesting they ride together. Having only been stationed there three months, he felt it would be a good opportunity to get to know each other better. A1C Burroughs got into SSgt. Steffens vehicle and they continued to patrol the perimeter. They decided to check the East Gate in order to ensure it was secure because there was no guard stationed there on the weekends.

East Gate of RAF Woodbridge

At 11:50 on December 26, as they were patrolling near the East Gate of RAF Woodbridge, SSgt. Steffens observed strange red and blue lights in the sky directly above the trees of nearby Rendlesham Forest. He pointed to the sky and asked A1C Burroughs if that was normal or if he had ever seen lights such as these anywhere off the base. When A1C Burroughs looked, he replied that he had never observed anything like it before. By this time, the unusual lights appeared to be descending into the forest.

SSgt. Steffens decided they should go drive into Rendlesham Forest in order to get a closer look. Without first reporting the incident to the Law Enforcement desk, he instructed A1C Burroughs to unlock the padlock on the East Gate. They proceeded to drive east until reaching a T-junction where SSgt. Steffens stopped and turned the car around so it was facing towards the East Gate in case they had to leave quickly. As they exited the vehicle, they noticed static electricity in the air. They observed a large, glowing, white light at the edge of the forest, and red and blue lights deep within the trees. SSgt. Steffens decided it would be best not to continue into the forest as it could be a possible security situation. He insisted that they drive back to the East Gate and call it in to the Law Enforcement desk.

Back at the East Gate, A1C Burroughs used the landline as opposed to his radio which might not have been secure, to report the strange lights to Sgt. "Crash" McCabe at the Law Enforcement desk. Sgt. "Crash" McCabe also asked to also speak with SSgt. Steffens concerning the incident. He then transferred the call to SSgt. John Coffey, Security Controller at Bentwaters who in turn alerted Central Security Flight Shift Commander Lt. Fred Buran.

Call to SSgt. James Penniston

At 12:02 a.m. while in the chow hall getting ready to have dinner with Sgt. McCulley, SSgt. Donnie Dillard at Central Security Control radioed SSgt. Penniston requesting that he call him via a land line. He informed him that he needed to go to the East Gate and rendezvous with two Flight C Law Enforcement officers. When SSgt. Penniston inquired as to what was going on, he was told that Lt. Fred Buran would rather he just go there and investigate. He asked if it could wait awhile as they were just about to have their dinner, but was told it was important that he leave now. They would brief him when he arrived and it was imperative that he use the phone and stay off the open airways.

At 12:06 a.m. SSgt. Penniston arrived at the East Gate. SSgt. Steffens remarked that he wasn't going to believe what he was about to see as he pointed down the East Gate road towards Rendlesham Forest where a dome of bright white light was over the trees. SSgt. Penniston's first impression was that it was a downed aircraft because he also saw orange, red, and blue glowing lights which was typical with aircraft crashes and Titanium fuel burning. Being so close to the runway, perhaps an aircraft had attempted to land, but experienced problems. He asked SSgt. Bud Steffens if he had heard it go down. He said there had been no sound and believed it had landed. Still certain that an aircraft had crashed, SSgt. Penniston called Central Security Control from the phone at the Gate, not using the radio because there was a chance this could be classified, and asked to speak to Master Sergeant J. D. Chandler who was the Flight Chief for both bases.

At 12:15 a.m. MSgt. Chandler instructed him to wait while he contacted Bentwaters control tower in regards to any suspicious aircraft activity in the area. Bentwaters operators in turn contacted British airfields RAF Watton in Norfolk, RAF Bawdsey in Suffolk, and Heathrow Airport in London. Reporting back to MSgt. Chandler, the consensus was that all three radar operators had observed an uncorrelated object moving at thousands of miles per hour for fifteen minutes until it disappeared over Woodbridge. With what appeared to be of great importance, he contacted Colonel Ted Conrad the Base Commander for permission to conduct a first response off base in order to investigate what might be a downed aircraft in Rendlesham Forest and received clearance allowing SSgt. Penniston and two patrolmen to proceed on foot.

SSgt. Penniston requested MSgt. Chandler's assistance since they would be searching Rendlesham Forest located within British territory. SSgt. Steffens said he would remain at the East Gate until he arrived. The men would radio information from the forest to MSgt. Chandler at the East Gate who would in turn contact Central Security Control.

At 12:30 a.m. SSgt. Jim Penniston, A1C Ed Cabansag, and A1C John Burroughs got into the jeep and drove down East Gate Road to a logging track leading into the forest. The dome of light began to appear brighter reinforcing the idea there was a fire deep within the woods most likely from a downed aircraft. Upon reaching the end of the road, they came to an open field. Before them were frozen berms, natural ridges, and ditches so deep that they came to realize it would be too dangerous to drive the jeep any further. They had no choice but to disembark and continue on foot.

They proceeded and at 12:51 a.m. all their radios began to exhibit interference and signal failure. Not wanting to risk losing communication with MSgt. Chandler, SSgt. Penniston appointed A1C Cabansag to hold his location back by the jeep and act as a relay while he and A1C Burroughs moved on.

SSgt. Jim Penniston

A1C John Burroughs

A1C Ed Cabansag

As the two men continued on a south-easterly direction into the woods, the atmosphere began to change. The area seemed void of sound and the air contained a strange energy about it as they experienced a tingling sensation on their skin. There was a sense of slowness as if they were walking through water and it seemed like time itself was an effort.

They stopped momentarily, thinking they heard a woman's voice, but realized it was the sound of a distressed Muntjac deer which in turn was followed by the movement of animals in the foliage, and the intense sound of birds flapping their wings. Moments later, the ground began to tremor as animals ran past them moving quickly in the opposite direction. Were the animals fleeing from what they were soon to encounter?

By 1:00 a.m. they reached a point where they could observe a bright, yellow and white dome of light coming from a mechanical object on the ground. In addition, there was a red pulsating light above it and a blue and white light shining below. From there on, the landscape was more berms that were four to five feet in height and about ten feet apart. At 1:15 a.m. SSgt. Penniston instructed A1C Burroughs to wait while he approached the first of two berms.

After getting around the first one, he began to climb the second and looked over the side. There it was twenty feet away situated between two berms, a dark mechanical object looming from within the glowing light. As he looked on, a bright flash of blue and white light blinded him and he instinctively hit the ground for cover thinking the craft was exploding.

"Was it a signal, a warning, or a method of communication?"

As he lay there he contemplated that if that was an explosion why was there no sound? He looked back and noticed that A1C Burroughs had also climbed the berm and was approximately twenty feet behind him. He seemed to be engulfed in a bright beam of blue and white light that appeared to be shining down on him. He called out to him, but A1C Burroughs merely stood there with his arms at his side as if in a trance. Although he was concerned, he was more concerned about the physical effects of what was happening in the area. This craft could be highly radioactive and affecting both of them. With that, his main thought was the security of the base. Was this a threat?

As he looked at the black triangular craft, it was immediately apparent to him that this was not a crash site but a landing, nor was it any aircraft of which he was familiar. He was a trained aircraft observer and crash investigator having studied both the NATO and WARSHAW PACT aircraft and this craft was nothing like anything he had ever seen. Hoping the transmission went through, he radioed the base to terminate the Emergency Response and change it to Helping Hands meaning a hostile security situation may exist. Although he was not receiving any response, it was imperative he continue to transmit in hopes they were receiving his messages.

When he got to within ten feet of the craft, the area felt odd as if it was out of sync with the rest of the forest. The bright dome of light had dissipated and the only lights were blue and yellow coming from under the craft and swirling around the exterior. There was the smell of hot metal such as when an aircraft engine shuts down. He estimated the triangular craft to be about nine feet long and eighteen feet tall.

Reaching for his camera, he began taking photos. As he moved closer, he had already taken all thirty-six pictures of 35mm monochrome film. He slowly approached the craft noticing the surface was like a smooth, opaque, black glass with flickering lights that flashed from blue, to black to grey.

Moving his hand over the surface he could feel a continuous surge of low voltage electricity running through his hand and radiating up to his forearm. It would appear the craft was running, but there was no audible sound. The surface was about 20 degrees warmer than the 32 degree temperature that night. There were no flaps, intake, exhaust, or crew compartment. While inspecting underneath, there was no landing gear and yet it appeared to be resting off the ground about eighteen inches. Upon closer look, he discovered it was being supported by three beams of light.

He looked for any identifying markings such as USAF or NASA, but there were none. On the left side towards the front were five symbols, like glyphs, measuring about three inches high and extending a length of two feet across, and a larger symbol centrally placed above them. Slowly, he traced his hand over each symbol which felt slightly engraved. Then he opened his hand and pressed his palm over the large symbol that looked like a triangle within a circle. As he did so, the light at the top of the craft grew brighter, so bright that he could no longer see or hear. He began seeing a stream of intense blue and white light in his mind. Then the flickering light changed into a very fast sequence of zeros and ones in black and white.

Once he was able to see again, he noticed it was now 2:30 a.m. and he found himself standing next to Burroughs who had been relieved of the suspended state he had been put in. This was strange as he was sure it had only been about twenty minutes. How could he account for the missing time? Had his movements slowed while inside the light? Moreover, how was he now suddenly standing next to A1C Burroughs who had been twenty feet away?

They noticed the craft began to turn a vivid, bright, white color. Thinking it was going to explode, they backed away to a safe distance. It began to lift up slowly about three feet with no sound or air disturbance. Then it started to move slowly weaving back and forth through the trees until it was able to maneuver to a distance of about 100-150 feet, before it rose up over the trees about 200 feet, and disappeared at an impossible speed.

SSgt. Penniston thought the craft was gone. However, A1C Burroughs pointed to the sky where he observed it again about 400 yards to the east. They began running towards it and in a few minutes came out the other side of the forest. The craft was now beyond the Capel Green farm. They climbed over the wire fence, chasing it, and watching as it would disappear and then reappear. They finally stopped pursuit about 300 yards east of the farmhouse.

The radio began to work again. SSgt. Penniston reported to SSgt. Coffey that they were catching up with the craft that was doing strange maneuvers in the sky. SSgt. Coffey's main concern was if they were okay. When SSgt. Penniston confirmed that they were, SSgt. Coffey said he was terminating the investigation. They were to report to MSgt. Chandler when they arrived back at the East Gate.

On their way back through the forest, they returned to the clearing where the craft had landed. A1C Burroughs noticed three indentations in the ground made by the strange "landing gear." Each was about seven inches wide and two inches deep. They planned to return in the morning in order to examine the site better. As they headed back, they met up with A1C Cabansag who had been waiting by the Jeep and drove back to the East Gate.

After arriving back at the East Gate at Woodbridge, they noticed the van that was waiting for them that would take them back to Bentwaters. SSgt. Penniston met with his team and A1C Burroughs met with the Law Enforcement Patrol.

SSgt. Penniston boarded the van and while waiting for everyone else to board, took out his notebook. He began a short summary of what had happened preparing for the official AF1569 form that would then be entered into the Security blotter. He made sure not to mention the fact about his up close inspection of the craft and especially about the word "UFO." That would most certainly put an end to his career. A1C Richard Bertalino from Flight C sat down next to him and they talked briefly. He asked how close he had gotten to the craft. SSgt. Penniston smiled and replied, "Too close … way too close." Then he reached for his notebook and did a quick sketch.

Upon arriving at Bentwaters, MSgt J. D. Chandler, the Deputy Base Commander, was standing there awaiting their arrival. SSgt. Penniston looked at him and said, "You're not going to believe what happened tonight." Msgt. Chandler assured him that he would indeed because he had seen everything from the East Gate. He said everyone had been worried about them because they had lost all contact with them for approximately three hours. SSgt. Penniston attributed that to the fact that the radios for some reason had just stopped picking up a signal. Just then, he looked at his watch that read 4:15 a.m. He was surprised to learn according to everyone else it was actually 5:00 … 45 minutes were missing.

"I left the forest a different man"

The following day, SSgt. Penniston continued to be awakened with visions of sequences of zeros and ones flashing through his mind. He realized these images were the result of his touching the symbols on the craft. Although these numbers had no meaning to him at the moment, he felt compelled to record them in his notebook along with drawings of the craft and the symbols.

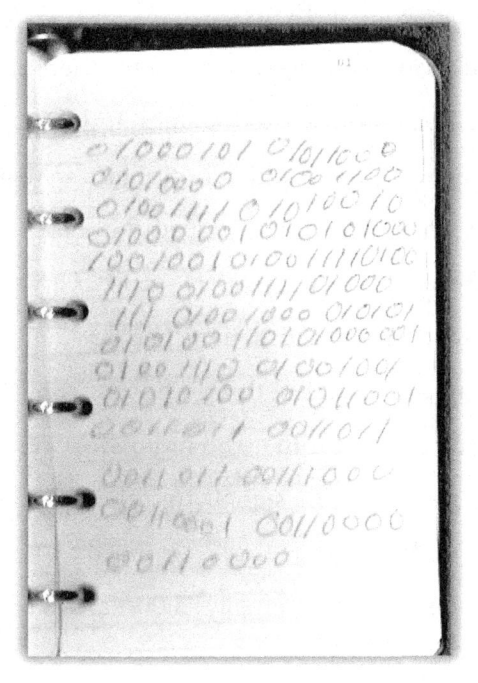

Binary Code page 1 of 16

Chosen

"A fireball was in front of me!"

On December 27, Private Lori Buoen age 18 of D-Flight team was on guard duty at the East Gate. Usually the team worked the afternoon shifts that ended at 9:00 p.m. However, tonight she was asigned the midnight shift. Although she didn't know, there was a reason she was assigned the gate with the view of the forest; the forest where the previous night SSgt. Penniston, A1C Buroughs, and A1C Casansag had an experience.

About 2:00 a.m. while inside the sentry box, she observed a huge fireball just north of the darkened runway and above Rendlesham Forest. She described it as, "If you took three handfuls of colored fire, put them together, and saw one color, then another, and another, you would get the impression that they were not flickering, but turning." Then she watched as it slowly descended into the forest and disappeared.

Immediately, she reached for the phone inside the wooden sentry box to notify Law Enforcement about what she had seen and asked for assistance. Cpl. John Trementozzi of Police 5 responded. He and three other police had been checking along the runways when they too noticed lights in the sky.

The two of them observed, red, green, and white lights in the northern sky. It wasn't the lighthouse because that was in the east. The lights were not flashing like stars, but steady. They would be in one place and then disappear, move to another place and reappear, and do it again. There was no particular pattern to the movement. This continued for another hour and a half until 3:30. a.m.

Private Lori Buoen   Corporal John Trementozzi
Law Enforcement Police 5

Soon they heard a transmission come over his Motorola police radio. It was the distressed voice of Lt. Bonnie Tramplin, Shift Commander D-Flight. Unbeknownst

Chosen

to them after receiving Private Buoen's report of a fireball, Cpl. Tramplin and MSgt. Robert Ball drove to the forest to investigate. "Bob, Bob! Where are you. I can't see anything!" she exclaimed as a strange light entered her vehicle.

Lieutenant Bonnie Tramplin
Shift Commander D-Flight

The Debrief

Major Edward Drury was the Deputy Squadron Commander to Major Malcolm Zickler who was in command of the 81st Security Police and Law Enforcement Squadron. He and Captain Mike Verrano, on duty shift commander the morning after the incident, both conducted debriefings with

SSgt. Penniston and A1C Burroughs. With these reports and confirmation that a UFO had been tracked on radar at the Bentwaters Command Post, they made the decision to investigate the landing site themselves.

They contacted SSgt. Penniston and A1C Burroughs telling them to report back to the site in order to rendezvous with them. The two men drove back to the forest, got out of their vehicle, and continued on foot to the landing site. A1C Burroughs located the three indentations and SSgt. Penniston walked around measuring the distance between the marks.

Major Drury, Captain Verrano, MSgt. Ray Gulyas, who was to take measurements of the landing site and take photos, and Suffolk Policeman Brian Cresswell arived. After pointing out the area, SSgt. Penniston and A1C Burroughs returned home. The three officers explored the area a few minutes and returned to the base to brief Major Malcolm Zickler where they were instructed to rendezvous with Brian Creswell a British Policeman.

Capt. Mike Verrano & Suffolk Police Brian Creswell

Once SSgt. Penniston arrived back to his home in Ipswich, he realized he had too much on his mind to sleep. He was inclined to gather more evidence of his experience so he phoned a civilian friend and was able to get plaster of Paris, a jug of water, and a small bucket. Putting the items into his knapsack, he returned to Woodbridge and the landing site. Once there, he mixed the plaster, poured it into the three holes, and waited an hour while it set. He carefully removed the casts, wapped them in plastic, and put them inside the knapsack.

Just as he was leaving, Major Drury, Captain Verrano, MSgt. Gulyas, and Brian Creswell the British police officer arrived. They questioned him as to why he was there. Without revealing what was inside his knapsack, he simply remarked that he was attempting to better understand the events that had occurred by revisiting the landing site. Something inside him instilled a sense of mistrust that this event would be a cover-up. Major Drury informed him that they were going to further investigate. He need not be bothered with the investigation and should go home and sleep.

Before heading home, he dropped off the 35mm film canister at the base photo lab. He was looking forward to seeing the images of the craft that he had captured. However, he found it quite disconcerting when he was notified that when the film was developed the photos were fogged. Was the film damaged from radiation emitting from the craft? Or was the military confiscating the images?

Plaster cast of one the holes at the landing site

Chosen

"An airman was taken."

On December 27 at 4:00 p.m. Sgt. Monroe Nevilles, Disaster Preparedness Technician at Bentwaters received a surprise visit at his residence from Lt. Bruce Englund Shift Commander for the Security Police on B Flight. He informed him that he was there under secret direct orders from Base Commander Colonel Ted Conrad.

Sgt. Nevilles was to immediately accompany Lt. Eglund in order to investigate the supposed landing site at which on December 26, SSgt. Penniston, A1C Burroughs, and A1C Cabansag had an encounter with a craft of unknown origin in the Rendlesham Forest. Moreover, Colonel Conrad told Lt. Englund that, "an airman had been taken" that night.

As Lt. Englund briefed Sgt. Neville along the way, the two men headed to the forest with an AN/PVS-2 Starlight nightvision scope designed for night combat capable of detecting infra-red light and a Kodak Tri-X camera pushed to ASA 800. Once at the landing site, they found three indentations in the ground, which they measured and photographed. They continued to investigate until about 7:00 p.m., got back into the Jeep, and headed to the East Gate of Bentwaters. On the way, Sgt. Neville looked over his left shoulder and saw a bright light. Through his nightvision goggles, he could see it was a green light; very green around the outside, but the dark center looked like the pupil of an eye. It began pulsating as if the "eye" was blinking. They stopped the Jeep and Sgt. Nevilles got out. At this point the light became brighter and he could feel static electricity above his head. He opened the door to get back into the vehicle and the light appeared to dim. However, when he attempted to open the door again, the light became brighter as if it was reacting to his movements.

Once back at base, they went to the Officers Club where a Christmas party was underway. They discussed their findings with Col. Conrad, the base commander of the twin airfields, who asked if they considered it warranted further investigation. When Sgt. Nevilles said it did, Col. Halt immediately began to assemble a team to investigate.

Halt Investigation

The following night Col. Halt and Sgt. Monroe Nevilles, a Disaster Preparedness Technician trained and certified by the Air Force and Marine Corps in nuclear, chemical, and biological detection equipment, returned to the forest. With them were Lt. Bruce Englund, MSgt. Bobby

Ball, SSgt. Adrian Bustinza, and Security Police Chief Malcolm Zickler.

Col. Halt carried a hand held analog recorder on which he intermittemtly recorded the investigation. Four years later in July 1984 the eighteen minute tape was released to the public.

With gas-powered light-all searchlights, the men walked into the forest until they came 150 feet from the suspected impact site. Just as the previous night, they began to experience equipment failures when the light-alls began to malfunction.

They approached three indentations in the frozen ground that formed an exact equlaterial triangle. Sgt. Nevilles used an AN-PDR-27F Radiac that furnishes visual and audible detection to test for any Beta and Gamma radiation. No Beta was evident, but Gamma of .7 milliroentgens was present in the three depressions, near the center of the triangle formed by the depressions, and on the side of the trees toward the depressions. In the center of the triangle was what appeared to be a small blast area. Upon further inspection, the indentations looked as though something dropped down and then twisted from side to side.

Looking up, they observed an opening in the trees with some freshly broken pine branches about an inch in diameter on the ground underneath. It appeared they came from about twenty feet up. A pine tree that faced into the blast of the assumed landing site had an abrasion facing that direction.

The abrasion was round, about 3 ½ inches in diameter, with crystalline pine sap that had come out fast. Halt instructed the men to take samples of the tree and sap. As they looked around, it was discovered that all the trees facing the center had similar elements. Sgt. Nevilles tested the abrasion and got readings of .5 on the geiger counter. However there were no readings on the back side of the tree.

Upon implementing the AN/PVS-2 Starlight nightvision scope, MSgt. Ball indicated there was a heat signature on the trees, facing the indentations, three or four feet off the ground in the area of the abrasion. Inside the triangle was a slight heat signature or some form of energy where some type of abrasion pushed the pine needles back. This was the same area where the high radioactive reading was detected.

At 1:48 a.m. the farm animals began to make strange noises. Up ahead they encountered a red light about 120 degrees on the compass from the site. The geiger counter began to register 4 clicks. Then the light disappeared, but came back at a compass reading of 110 degrees, about four feet off the ground. By now the farm animals were quiet and the atmosphere was strangely calm. The light began flashing from red to yellow as it approached their way. It appeared there were small particles of light shooting out from underneath. Now there were two lights with one on the left.

The men approached the lights that were about three hundred yards away, but now there was only one and it was pulsating. MSgt. Ball looked at it through the Starlight and remarked that it looked like an eye winking because it had a hollow dark center like a pupil.

They continued and finally after passing the farmer's house they reached a field. There they observed five red lights of similar shape that were steady instead of pulsating. At 2:44, they crossed the creek and were at the far side of the second farmer's field. A red-orange object was sitting in the field. A red light, sometimes flashing was observed at 110 degrees on the compass. Five clicks registered on the meter. At 3:05, at about ten degrees on the horizon, directly north, were two strange objects. They were elliptical shaped, making sharp angular movements and displayed red, green, and blue lights. The objects morphed into full circles for about a minute. At

3:15 a.m. an object appeared about ten degrees directly south. The ones to the north were now moving away from them at a high rate of speed. The light from the south began to come toward them and a beam was coming down to the ground. They continued to observe these objects until 3:30.

At 4:00, A1C Burroughs was given permission to enter the forest with Sgt. Bustinza. At this time, one bright object was still reported hovering over RAF Woodbridge at about ten degrees off the horizon. It was still moving erratically and similar lights were beaming down. The object then moved over the forest. The two men pursued the light into the forest until they reached a farmer's field. Sgt. Bustinza was suddenly blinded by a bright light and forced down to the ground. He looked to his right and saw that A1C Burroughs, standing motionless, was surrounded by a huge beam of red-orange light that appeared to be coming from above. Sgt. Bustinza called out to him, but he didn't respond. Later, A1C Burroughs mentioned experiencing missing time; the last thing he remembered was getting closer to a red-orange light. Was he "taken" again?

RAF Watton Radar

In Norfolk, The RAF Watton logbook entry dated 28 December 1980 and time at 0325 GMT: "Bentwaters Command Post contacted Eastern Radar and requested information of aircraft in the area UA37 traffic southbound FL370 – UFO sightings at Bentwaters. They are taking action."

UA37 traffic was the code for an air corridor uased by civilian aircraft which ran north-south for approximately forty miles east of RAF Bentwaters. FL370 signified "traffic" at 37,000 feet in altitude. 0325 GMT is consistant with the timing of Halt's investigation in Rendleshasm Forest where they observed lights in the sky. Interesting note: On December 29, U.S. Intelligence Operatives came to RAF Watton and took the radar-based data log book for the relevant time.

"Don't worry. We have it covered."

On the evening of December 28, Sgt. Rick Bobeau was stationed in the watchtower overlooking the WSA, Weapon Storage Area, where the nuclear weapons were stored. He had the ability to call a "Broken Arrow" if he noticed any intrusion of light down into the Weapon Storage Area. Broken Arrow is the code name that denotes a military ground unit is facing imminent danger from enemy attack and all available air forces within range are to provide air support immediately.

For ninety minutes, he observed a huge ball in the sky the size of a full moon, but it was firey red and blue just like Pvt. Lori Buoen had seen. As he looked at it through the crosshairs of his gun, it didn't move. Then little white lights dropped from it and descended into Rendlesham Forest.

He radioed Central Security Control who replied, "Don't worry. We have it covered." The light remained steady moving only once until again more little white lights dropped from it and descended into the forest. For the second time he radioed Central Security Control who once more replied, "Don't worry. We have it covered."

"It was traveling thousands of miles per hour!"

MSgt. Ike Barker second in charge at RAF Bentwaters and Jim Carey, were radar operators with the

Chosen

2164th Communications Squadron. About 11:00 p.m. on December 28 they were on duty in the Air Traffic control center. During this time as they watched the radar scope that covered a sixty mile radius around the Bentwaters complex, an unidentified object was tracked coming from the northeast direction and moving at an extremely high rate of speed. MSgt. Barker an eight year veteran was familiar with about every aircraft in the U.S., NATO, and Soviet, but not this.

The men watched as the object that had remarkable speed and maneuverability moved across their sixty mile scope covering 120 miles in a matter of a few seconds. It was estimated to be moving Mach 7 or 8 which was faster than anything they knew.

MSgt. Baker moved away from the radar screen and went outside in order to observe the object first hand. As he watched, it moved closer, slowed down, and then hovered over the base's water tower. The craft was at an altitude of between 1,500 and 2,000 feet. It was basketball size, orange in color with portholes around the center from which lights were emanating outward. The craft hovered for a few seconds, made an unnatural right angle shift, and departed at a high rate of speed. Once again it showed back on radar, hovered a few seconds, and entered Randlesham Forest at the same time Col. Halt and his team were investigating.

Cheryl Lynn Carter

Statement A1C Edward N. Cabansag

A1C Ed Cabansag maintains that he was strongly encouraged to sanitize the events in his statement.

"On 26 December 80, SSgt Penniston and I were on Security #6 at Woodbridge Base. I was the member. We were patrolling Delta NAPA when we received a call over the radio. It stated that Police #4 had seen some strange lights out past the East Gate and we were to respond. SSgt. Penniston and I left Delta NAPA, heading for the East Gate code two. When we got there SSgt. Steffens and A1C Burroughs were on patrol. They told us they had seen some funny lights out in the woods. We notified CSC and we asked permission to investigate further. They gave us the go-ahead.

We left our weapons with SSgt. Steffens who remained at the gate. Then the three of us went out to investigate. We stopped the Security Police vehicle about 100 meters from the gate. Due to the terrain we had to go on by foot. We kept in constant contact with CSC. While we walked, each one of us would see the lights; blue, red, white, and yellow. The beacon light turned out to be the yellow light. We would see them periodically, but not in a specific pattern. As we approached, the lights would seen at be at the edge of the forest. We were about 100 meters from the edge of the forest when I saw a quick movement. It looked visible for a moment. It looked like it spun left a quarter of a turn, then it was gone. I advised SSgt. Penniston and A1C Burroughs. We advised CSC and proceeded in extreme caution. When we got about 50-75 meters, MSgt. Chandler/Flight Chief was on the scene. CSC was not reading our transmissions very well, so we used MSgt. Chandler as a go-between. He remained back at our vehicle.

As we entered the forest, the blue and red lights were not visible any more. Only the beacon light was still blinking. We figured the lights were coming from past the forest since nothing was visible when we passed through the woody forest. We would see a glowing near the beacon light, but as we got closer we found it to be a lit up farm house. After we had passed through the forest, we thought it had to be an aircraft accident. So did CSC as well. But we ran and walked a good two miles past our vehicle until we got to a vantage point where we could determine that what we were chasing was only a beacon of light off in the distance. Our route through the forest and field was a direct one straight towards the light. We informed CSC that the light beacon was farther than we thought so CSC terminated our investigation. A1C Burroughs and I took a road while SSgt. Penniston walked straight back from where we came,. A1C Burroughs saw the light again. This time it was coming from the left of us as we were walking back to the vehicle. We got in contact SSgt. Penniston and we took a walk through where we saw the lights. Nothing. Finally, we made it back to our vehicle after making contact with the BC's and informing them of what we saw. After that we met MSgt. Chandler and we went in service again after termination of the sighting."

Statement and Drawing A1C John Burroughs

"On the night 25-26 December at around 0300 while on patrol down at east gate, myself and patrol saw lights coming from the woods due east of the gate. The lights were red and blue, the red one above the blue one, and they were flashing on and off. Because I've never seen anything like that coming from the woods before we decided to drive down and see what it was. We went down east gate road and took a right at the stop sign and drove down about 10-20 yards to where there is a road that goes into the forest. At the road I could see a white light shining onto the trees and I could still see the red and blue lights. We decided we better go call it in so we went back up towards east gate. I was watching the lights and the white light started coming down the road that led into the forest. We got to the gate and called it in. The whole time I could see the lights and the white light was almost at the edge of the road and the blue and red lights were still out in the woods. A security unit was sent down to the gate and when they got there they could see it too. We asked for permission to go and see what it was and they told us we could. We took the truck down the road that lead into the forest. As we went down the east gate road and the road that lead into the forest the lights were moving back and they appeared to stop in a bunch of trees.

We stopped the truck where the road stopped and went in on foot. We crossed a small open field that lead into the trees where the lights were coming from and as we were coming into the trees, it sounded like a woman was screaming. Also the woods lit up and you could hear the farm animals making a lot of noise. And there was a lot of movement in the woods. All three of us hit the ground and whatever it was started moving back towards the open field. We got up to a fence that separated the trees from the open field and you could see the lights down by the farmer's house. We climbed over the fence and started heading towards the red and blue lights and they just disappeared. Once we reached the farmer's house we could see a beacon going around so we went towards it. We followed it for about two miles before we could see it was coming from a light house. We had just crossed a creak and were told to come back when we saw a blue light to our left on the trees. It was only there for a minute and it just streaked away. After that, we didn't see anything so we returned to the truck."

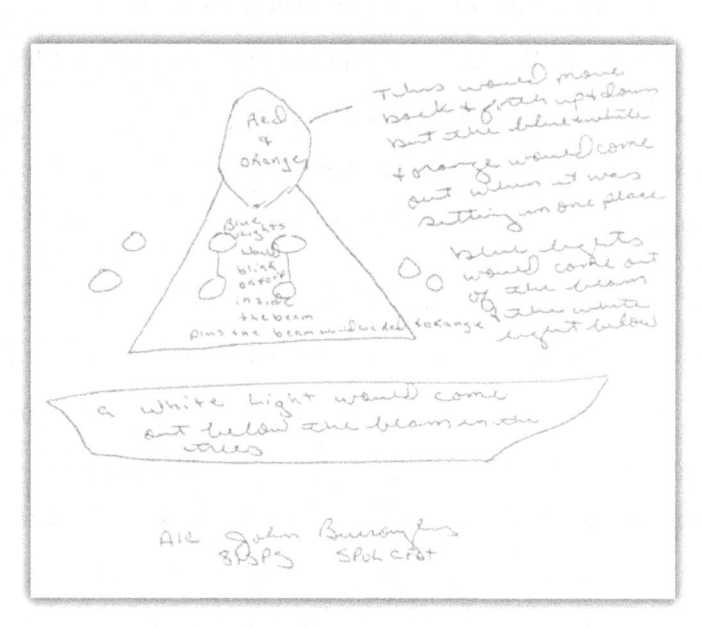

AIC John Burroughs Drawing

Chosen

Statement and Drawing SSgt. Jim Penniston

When he was asked to write his statement, the original was four written legal pages. However upon arriving at the Air Force Office of Special Investigations, AFOSI, two men in black suits handed him this typed unsigned and undated statement saying, "We're in charge of this and this is what you tell anybody that asks."

"Received dispatch from CSC to rendezvous with Police 4 A1C Burroughs, and Police 5 SSgt. Steffens at east gate Woodbridge. Upon arriving, at east gate directly to the east about 1 ½ miles in a large wooded area, a large yellow glowing light was emitting above the trees. (see diagram). In the centre of the lighted area directly in the center of the ground level, there was a red light blinking on and off 5 to 10 second intervals. And a blue light that was being for the most part steady. After receiving permission from CSC, we proceeded off base past east gate, down an old logging road. Left vehicle, proceeded on foot. Burroughs and I were approximately 15-20 meters apart and proceeding on a true east direction from logging road. The area in front of us was lighting up a 30 meter area. When we got within a 50 meter distance, the object was producing red and blue light. The blue light was steady and projecting under the object. It was up the area directly extending a meter or two out. At this point of positive identification I relayed to CSC, SSgt. Coffey. Positive sighting of the object ... 1... color of lights and that it was definitely mechanical in nature. This is the closest point that I was near the object at any point. We then proceeded after it. It moved in a zig-zagging manner back through the woods, then lost sight of it. On the way back we encountered a blue streaking light to the left only lasting a few seconds. After a 45 minute walk, we arrived at our vehicle."

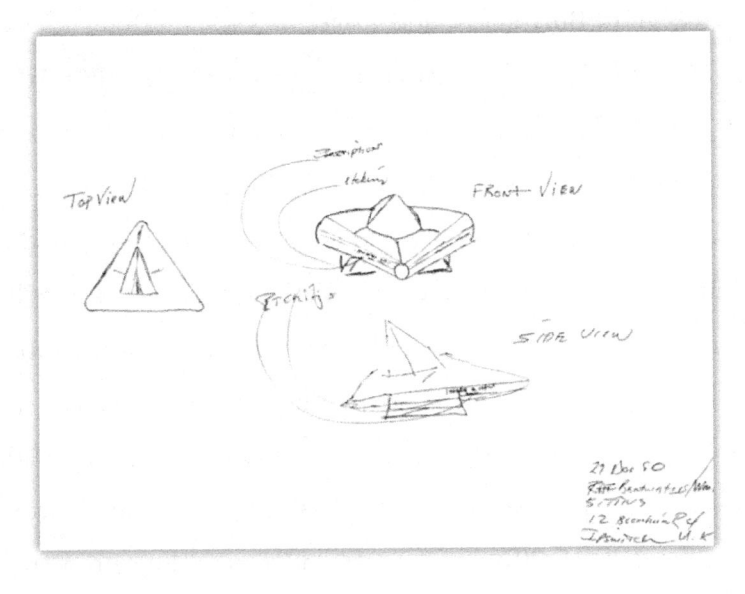

Sgt. Jim Penniston's Drawing of the Craft

Chosen

STATEMENT

Received dispatch from CSC to rendzvous with Police 4 A1C Burroughs, and Police 5 SSgt Seffens at east gate Woodbridge. Upon arriving at east gate directly to the east about 1 ½ miles in a large wooded area. A large yellow glowing light was emitting above the trees.(refer diagram) In the center of the lighted area directly in the center ground leval, there was a red light blinking on and off 5 to 10 sec intervals. And a blue light that was being for the most part steady. After receiving permission from CSC, we proceeded off base pass east gate, down an old logging road. Left vehicle proceeded on foot . Bonroughs and I were approx. 15-20 meters apart and procseding on a true east direction. from the logging road. The area in front of us was lighting up a 30 meter area. When we got with in a 50 meter distance. The object was producing red and bl ue light. The blue light was steady and projecting under the object. It was lighting up the area directly under IIIexstending a meter or two out. At this point of positive identification I relayed to CSC, SSgt Coffey. Postitive siming of object...l..color of lights and that it was defidently mechaniclal in nature. This is the closes point that I was near the objet at any point. We then proceeded after it. It moved in a zig-zagging manner back through the woni then lost site of it. On the way back we encounterd a blue streaking light to left lasting only a few seconds. After a 45 min wal k arrived at our vehicle.

Typed Statement Revised by the Men in Black

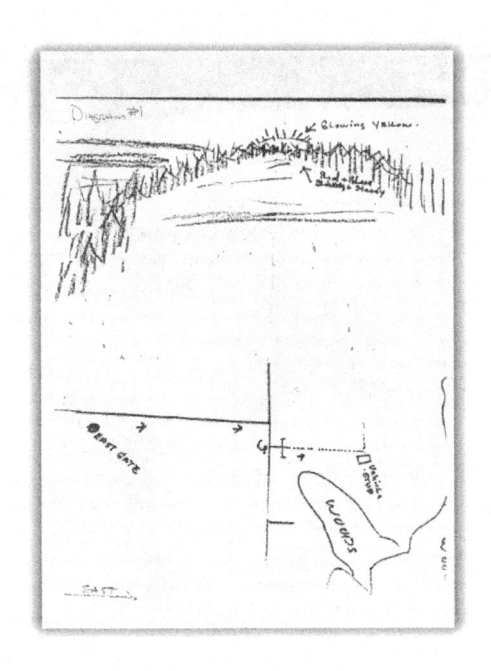

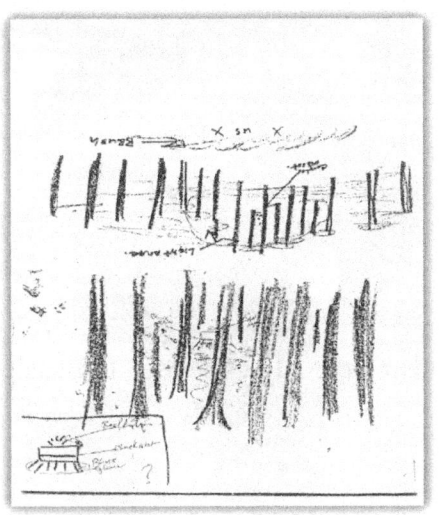

Map of Rendlesham Forest in Regards to the Craft

Halt Memo

On January 13, 1981, Lieutenant Colonel Charles Halt, the Deputy Base Commander at RAF Bentwaters, prepared a Memo which he sent to the U.K. Ministry of Defense: Subject – Unexplained lights.

Department of the Air Force
Headquarters Combat Support Group (USAFC)
APO New York

Early in the morning of 27 Dec 80 (approximately (300L), two USAF security police patrolmen saw unusual lights outside the back gate at RAF Woodbridge. Thinking an aircraft might have crashed or been forced down, they call for permission to go outside the gate to investigate. The on-duty flight chief responded and allowed three patrolmen to proceed on foot. The individuals reported seeing a strange glowing object in the forest. The object was described as being metallic in appearance and triangular in shape, approximately two meters high. It illuminated the entire forest with a white light. The object itself had a pulsing red light on top and a bank (s) of blue lights underneath. The object was hovering or on legs. As the patrolmen approached the object, it maneuvered through the trees and disappeared.

At this time the animals on a nearby farm went into a frenzy. The object was briefly sighted approximately an hour later near the back gate.

The next day, three depressions 1 ½" deep and 7" in diameter were found where the object had been sighted on the ground. The following night (29 Dec 80) the area was checked for radiation. Beta/Gamma readings of 0.1 milliroentgens were recorded with peak reading in the three depressions and near the center of the triangle formed by the depressions. A nearby tree had moderate (.05-.07) readings on the side of the tree toward the depressions.

Later in the night a red sun-like light was seen through the tree. It moved about and pulsed. At one point it appeared to throw off glowing particles and then broke into five separate white objects and then disappeared. Immediately thereafter, three star-like objects were noticed in the sky. Two objects to the north and one to the south, all of which were about 10 degrees off the horizon. The objects moved rapidly in sharp angular movements and displayed red, green, and blue lights. The objects to the north appeared to be elliptical through an 8-12 power lens. They then turned to full circles. The object to the south was visible for two or three hours and beamed down a stream of light from time to time.

Numerous individuals, including the undersigned, witnessed the activities in paragraphs 1 and 2.

> Charles I. Halt. Lt. Col. USAF
> Deputy Base Commander

Halt said, "He may have been abducted. Who knows? We do know that there was lost time (45 minutes). They were not on the radio. We had men out in the forest that were unaccounted for hours.

I believe the objects that I saw at close quarter were extraterrestrial in origin, maybe not a being as we know, maybe an entity that has intelligence, and that the security services of both the United States and the United Kingdom have attempted, both then and now, to subvert the significance of what occurred at Rendlesham Forest and RAF Bentwaters by the use of well-practiced methods of disinformation."

Cheryl Lynn Carter

> **DEPARTMENT OF THE AIR FORCE**
>
> CD 13 Jan 81
>
> SUBJECT: Unexplained Lights
>
> TO: RAF/CC
>
> 1. Early in the morning of 27 Dec 80 (approximately 0300L), two USAF security police patrolmen saw unusual lights outside the back gate at RAF Woodbridge. Thinking an aircraft might have crashed or been forced down, they called for permission to go outside the gate to investigate. The on-duty flight chief responded and allowed three patrolmen to proceed on foot. The individuals reported seeing a strange glowing object in the forest. The object was described as being metalic in appearance and triangular in shape, approximately two to three meters across the base and approximately two meters high. It illuminated the entire forest with a white light. The object itself had a pulsing red light on top and a bank(s) of blue lights underneath. The object was hovering or on legs. As the patrolmen approached the object, it maneuvered through the trees and disappeared. At this time the animals on a nearby farm went into a frenzy. The object was briefly sighted approximately an hour later near the back gate.
>
> 2. The next day, three depressions 1 1/2" deep and 7" in diameter were found where the object had been sighted on the ground. The following night (29 Dec 80) the area was checked for radiation. Beta/gamma readings of 0.1 milliroentgens were recorded with peak readings in the three depressions and near the center of the triangle formed by the depressions. A nearby tree had moderate (.05-.07) readings on the side of the tree toward the depressions.
>
> 3. Later in the night a red sun-like light was seen through the trees. It moved about and pulsed. At one point it appeared to throw off glowing particles and then broke into five separate white objects and then disappeared. Immediately thereafter, three star-like objects were noticed in the sky, two objects to the north and one to the south, all of which were about 10° off the horizon. The objects moved rapidly in sharp angular movements and displayed red, green and blue lights. The objects to the north appeared to be elliptical through an 8-12 power lens. They then turned to full circles. The objects to the north remained in the sky for an hour or more. The object to the south was visible for two or three hours and beamed down a stream of light from time to time. Numerous individuals, including the undersigned, witnessed the activities in paragraphs 2 and 3.
>
> CHARLES I. HALT, Lt Col, USAF
> Deputy Base Commander

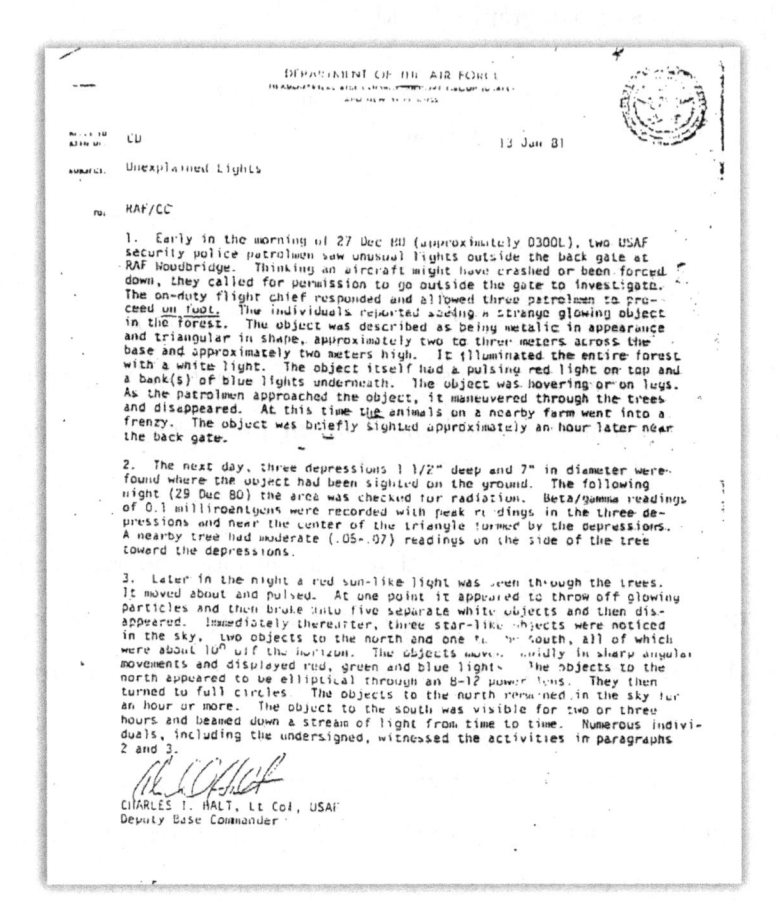

Halt Memo

Jim Penniston Returns to the U.S.

Jim Penniston returned to the United States in May 1994 leaving the memory of Rendlesham Forest behind.

However, it would appear that Rendlesham Forest still lingered somewhere deep within his subconscious mind. The dreams would come; dreams that quickly morphed into nightmares that prevented him from getting a good night's sleep.

His physician referred him to a therapist. After several appointments and attempts with medications to assist with his sleep disorder, her assessment was that it was most likely attributed to a traumatic experience in his past and possibly during childhood. She suggested he undergo hypnotic regression beginning from his first childhood memories to adulthood.

On August 26, 1994, she conducted a regression. After waking up from an hour and a half session, he didn't remember anything he had said, but he felt more relaxed. On the other hand as he looked at the therapist, she had a rather strange look on her face and was overly quiet. She looked down at her notepad and finally said, "Tell me about RAF Woodbridge."

She continued by saying that everything from his childhood to adulthood seemed normal until they came to his military career. It was obvious that the trauma in question was from his mid-twenties at this place known as RAF

Woodbridge. Now they would have to conduct another session in order to address that. Moreover, she was convinced that he had contact with something extraordinary and possibly other-worldly. She also remarked that something peculiar came up during the session; missing time. He had described standing near the craft, examining it, and then suddenly he was standing thirty feet away and next to John Burroughs. How were forty-five minutes missing?

Second Regression

Jim was eager for the next session as his dreams had now become more intense.

Hypnotist: "Let's go back to the craft and when you're feeling the symbols. What happens?"

Jim: "There's a bright light … gotta squint … I see the symbols, but not on … they're not on the craft."

Hypnotist: "Where are the symbols?"

Jim: "Inside."

Hypnotist: "Inside the craft?"

Jim: "No, in my head."

Hypnotist: "How did they get inside your head?"

Jim: "I don't know … it's awful bright."

Hypnotist: "And the symbols are still in your head?"

Jim: "Different ones … I don't know what they mean … I feel safe … I don't know what is going on … that light … everywhere I look I see that …How can it be so bright?"

Hypnotist: "Did you get a sense that there was an entity attached to the symbols?"

Jim: "Yeah … communication."

Hypnotists: "Do you want to?"

Jim: "Want to! …I don't understand them … I don't understand … I'm safe though."

Hypnotist: "Can you ask the entity who put the symbols in your mind to tell you what they mean?"

Jim: "Can't do that … there's no people there … a machine."

Hypnotist: "Did you get the sense that a person or a living being projected these symbols to you?"

Jim: "I don't know, but I think so … they … there's too many of them … too many symbols to remember … they're so fast … flashing … I'm supposed to understand it though … I can't understand."

Hypnotist: "Where are you physically?"

Jim: "I'm outside … lights gone … I feel better though … I walk away … I pick up my camera from the ground. About twenty feet or so … that's when I heard John …I don't understand. What I remember is … I don't know."

Hypnotist: "What do you remember?"

Jim smiles: "A nursery rhyme! … Mary had a little lamb, its fleece was white as snow, and everywhere Mary went the lamb was sure to go."

Hypnotist: "What was that connected with?"

Jim: "The ship … I was told that … I was told I wasn't supposed to talk about that … I want out of here, I know that,"

Hypnotist: "Out of where?"

Jim: "That room … over at Bentwaters … I was told to go there … December 30."

Hypnotist: "Who taught that nursery to you?"

Jim: "I'm not sure. It wasn't the ship ... that was all symbols ... I can't tell the truth ... I was told not to tell the truth."

Hypnotist: "Who told you that?"

Jim: "The man in the room ... I was given a cup of coffee ...two agents were asking questions ... OSI Agents ... Burns ... Gallagher ... We seen something we weren't supposed to see."

Hypnotist: "Who decided you weren't supposed to see?"

Jim: "They decide that ... not the OSI ... those two other guys in the room ... they don't have names ... they're British agents ... DS8? C8? ... They're mad ... I'm lying to them ... but I'm not lying ... I can't tell anymore."

Hypnotist: "Why can't you tell anymore? What will happen if you tell them?"

Jim: "Punished ... the government will punish me ... jail ... I can never tell about it ...this is between us ... the OSI Agents and the other two ... It can't get out. It's not in the best interest of national security. There will be panic."

Hypnotist: "Who would panic? Why would they panic?"

Jim: "People ... they can't find out about them ... Them who made the craft."

Hypnotist: "Do the OSI people know them who made the craft?"

Jim: "No, the other two do ... one maybe Australian, the other isn't. The other is from London ... American."

Hypnotist: "Do you get the feeling, Jim that they know what you saw there?"

Jim: "The American does ... I don't know."

Hypnotist: "You don't know?"

Jim: "Oh, I know ... I just can't talk. Can't tell anybody."

Hypnotist: "Did they do something to you physically?"

Jim: "Yes ... That's why they gave it to me."

Hypnotist: "Gave it to you?"

Jim: "Shot ... Right in my arm ... hot."

Hypnotist: "When did the nursery rhyme come?"

Jim: "They told me about the nursery rhyme."

Hypnotist: "What does the nursery rhyme do?"

Jim: "Uh ... I can't talk about that."

Hypnotist: "Is the nursery rhyme a control … to give you a block?"

Jim: "It's a warning … I can't … I can't disobey the warning."

Hypnotist: "What would happen if you disobeyed the warning?"

Jim: "I don't know … bad, awful bad. Bad for me …and everybody else in the world. I would hurt everybody. It, it can't … I can't talk about it. I can't discuss that. It's too important."

Hypnotist: "Was there something that happened to you when you were by the craft before you went off with John that you can't talk about?"

Jim: "That's right. I can't talk about that.

Hypnotist: "So you can talk about what happened up to that point … of touching the …"

Jim: "Light!"

Hypnotist: "When the light came on … something happened?"

Jim: "Right."

Hypnotist: "And you can't talk about that?"

Jim: "Oh no… forbidden."

Hypnotist: "Can you describe what you see?"

Jim: "It's, it's a … I think I know why. I know why … It's not from outer space. No, no it belongs to us … It, no …that's impossible! I, I, I, don't really believe that."

Hypnotists: "Believe what?"

Jim: "They, they can't talk about it. Because it's us, it's us that's why."

Hypnotist: What's happening now?"

Jim: "I see the craft. The light dissipates. They, the Interrogators, want to know what symbols I'm seeing. I don't want to tell them, but I tell them … I said I felt the symbols because they were raised. Tell them about the lights. They already know about the lights. They are asking me if I see the Binary Code …I understand."

Hypnotist: "What do you understand?"

Jim: "I'm the interpreter. They need interpreters. The lights … You can't read these codes unless you have an interpreter. I understand what's going on now … The symbols, it's information being exchanged. That machine, that's for interpreters … there's lots of interpreters"

Hypnotist: Are you an interpreter?"

Jim: "Yes …Explain. Mission, Purpose … Mission is Contact, with us … Purpose is research, to help them."

Hypnotist: "To help them with what?"

Jim: "Themselves. They are time travelers. They are us … from the future … a very long time ago. They need something from all interpreters."

Hypnotist: "What do they need?"

Jim: "Not sure, but it has to do with chromosomes? Or something like that … They take it from other people's bodies."

Hypnotist: "Where did they take it from you?"

Jim: "Didn't … We only interrupted. They were interrupted. They are having problems. The program's… I understand what they are saying, but they weren't supposed to be there. They are having problems. The odds are against them."

Hypnotist: "You weren't supposed to understand the program?"

Jim: "No, by touching these things (symbols) I activated these things ... It was repairing itself. All they wanted was a place to stay while it repaired itself ... I activated a Binary Code. The two men, interrogators, want to know why."

Hypnotist: "And what do you answer them?"

Jim: "They ask if I ever had any other encounters with them. I haven't. They are discussing it between themselves. The situation ... they've got a problem. Their problem is because I can't tell anybody. They ask more questions about the craft. And they want to know what to do with me."

Hypnotist: "Do they ever take fetuses?"

Jim: "If it's tasked, they do. There are different ships for tasking. Everybody knows about this ... That's what they are talking about. That's why they want to contain the situation ... damage control."

Hypnotist: "Who has damage control? They see you as damage control?"

Jim: "The Americans and the British ... They see me and John, and they're worried about Colonel Halt. They know all about us."

Hypnotist: "Do they ever take chromosomes or cells or things from animals?"

Jim: "They have, but not for them ... to study. Sometimes they make different chemicals."

Hypnotist: "What would they make different chemicals for?"

Jim: "I don't know. They've had their problems, too. This time they were having problems, but they got it off. They have to be out in space to travel. I thought they just had to sit there. They've got to be in space. They need speed to travel."

Hypnotist: "To travel through time?"

Jim: "To go backwards. They can't go forward ... They go to their past. It's impossible to go into the future ... These ships can go forty or fifty thousand years. They can't go back much further. They might not be able to get back."

Hypnotists: "Have they had verbal contact with the government to explain this situation?"

Jim: "No, only through interpreters. That makes it hard for our government. They're not sure what the problem is. That's why I'm being debriefed."

Hypnotist: "Does the government believe what you are saying about them coming from the future?"

Jim: "Oh, yes."

Hypnotist: "Let's move forward to where you hear the agents talking about what they're going to do with you."

Jim: "They are going through their check list. They have a scripted check list. They tell me when I was at the East Gate with John they have five different stories to tell. Important to scramble dates. That's the unique thing about this. All stories are the same. They just have different dates … They are reading my story to me. The dates are just different. I'll remember. They're going to give me a warning. They tell me that I will hurt the world. It will breach national security and can destroy the system, cause wars, and chaos in the streets. That's why it's important to keep quiet."

John Burroughs Returns to the U.S.

After the strange encounter in Rendlesham, John Burroughs wasn't feeling well. The doctor at the base diagnosed him as having a virus. He was treated and later sent back to duty. Upon returning to the United States, he still didn't feel right. He had difficulty sleeping as his dreams conjured up memories; memories he couldn't remember when he awoke. Doctors diagnosed him with PTSD, Post

Traumatic Stress Disorder. His physician referred him to a therapist who attributed this to a traumatic experience. He suggested hypnotic regression and in 1988, he conducted a session.

Hypnotist: "Let's go back to Rendlesham Forest when you were with Col. Halt and you saw the blue lights."

John: "I told Col. Halt it's back again. He acted like he wasn't surprised. He was real calm. The other people were scared. They were surprised and very, very upset. Col. Halt was standing there. Arnold and I were standing there. We had things all around us ... above us. Col. Halt says they were making contact with someone."

"And I looked at him and said, 'What are you talking about?' He said well, they're out there. They've been out there for hours. The craft is still out. They're coming for that craft. They've been there for hours. I said I want to come closer."

"He said, 'Okay. You can come with, but Chris, I want you and Tommy to stay here. Get the light off the truck. John, I want you to go out there because I think you can bring this closer. I think you can bring this ship closer. They want you to do it."

Hypnotist: "Who wants you to do it?"

John: "Col. Halt said they did. All he said was they."

Hypnotist: "Did he appear to have some knowledge or some understanding you didn't understand?"

John: "I didn't understand what was going on."

Hypnotist: "He seemed to know something that you didn't?"

John: "He seemed to be very at peace of mind and very calm. He said this is the most bizarre, weirdest experience. People will never believe it."

Hypnotist: "Do you know why they thought you could bring it closer?"

John: "No, I did not understand. And that was something that I never understood either. They wanted me there and they wanted me in stages. You can stay in this area awhile. They weren't surprised that I was there either. They were not surprised. The people that saw me come out there were surprised, but Col. Halt was not surprised. And they kept me in stages. They kept me waiting like wait in here, wait in there, and now it's okay."

Hypnotist: "What happened then?"

John: "Well, then he put his arm around me and said let's go. All of a sudden, there was this short, dark suit, Mexican guy.

He was just there … he appeared. He appeared and he was coming up towards me. And he wasn't with the main group. He was like coming up towards me. And he said let's go. The three of us walked towards the craft. Col. Halt says, 'I got all this on tape recorder.' And he shows me his tape recorder. He has a radio with him too. 'I'm recording all this to Command Post where I'm going to keep all this stuff because it's going to be worth something.' And he said let's go and we started walking."

"The light was there. It was in the distance. And we walked a little farther and … THEN … there it was! … three blue lights!" Col Halt yells, "Was that there? We got that there! That's what we had before! John, you're not going to believe this, but the group of us, they made contact with us. They were on top of us. It's like they spoke to us."

"They? What's they? He said those lights. I mean you saw something. Those lights, they were right there and they were speaking to us. They were over us. They were flying in the sky. They were hovering over us. They were doing all kinds of things."

Hypnotist: "Okay, John. Hold it right there. I want you to look at one of those lights and ask it a question that comes to your mind. And that light will talk back to you. Tell me what it says."

John: "Come to me."

Hypnotist: "What did you do?"

John: "They started moving and we all froze. And they were up and down."

Hypnotist: "The lights?"

John: "Ya, they split up."

Hypnotist: "Okay, now ask them what they represent. Ask the light what it represents.'

John: "The craft."

Hypnotist: "Okay, is there any life form in or within that craft?"

John: "That was life form."

Although the regressions seemed to help alleviate the nightmares, he still didn't feel well physically. Since he couldn't go back to Woodbridge, they instructed him to go to an emergency room.

It was there where they discovered he had a heart murmur. He knew he did not have this condition previously because he would not have been able to enter the military. The base contacted Wright-Patterson Air Force Base in Ohio and he was sent there for an examination. The doctor ran several tests and confirmed that he had a heart murmur and an anomalous growth tissue in his heart. They didn't consider it serious at the time, but it worsened.

In 2012, John Burroughs attempted to link his congestive heart failure to a service connected disability. The Arizona Department of Veteran Affairs repeatedly denied him.

He turned to Senator John McCain's office for help. They filed for a copy of John's DD-214 Discharge in order to ascertain what his benefits were. However, they denied that he was in the military at that time. They said his DD-214 indicated he served from April, 14, 1982 – February 13, 1988. His tour at Woodbridge AFB was missing just like the missing time they experienced that night.

John Burroughs' attorney Pat Frascogna was finally able to obtain the original DD-214 showing him entering active duty in March 1979 and separated in April 1982. It was later discovered that his records along with Jim Penniston's, about a thousand pages, were legally classified. The records contain numerous references to Special Access Projects unrelated to Rendlesham.

In 2015, the United States government formally acknowledged the health issues of John Burroughs were the result of his encounter in Rendlesham Forest in December 1980. This decision granted him total medical disability by the Veterans Administration. It also recognizes the reality of such phenomenon and the possible health consequences. This set a precedent for other military members who have also experienced UFO encounters and suffered health issues. The cause of his injuries was determined to be broad-band non-ionizing electromagnetic radiation which is radio frequencies linked to cardiac injuries.

"Encounter in Rendlesham Forest" – Nick Pope with John Burroughs, USAF and Jim Patterson, USAF - 2015

"The Rendlesham Enigma" – Jim Penniston and Gary Osborn - 2019

Chapter 5
Mario Woods Incident

NORAD, North American Aerospace Defense Command, is located 200 feet below the Cheyenne Mountains in Colorado. The mission of this underground facility is Emergency Action Message dissemination in case of nuclear attack on the United States. They oversee the Northern Tier Defense System that includes Air Force Bases such as Ellsworth, SD; Minot, ND; Malmstrom, MT; Offutt, NB; and Francis E. Warren, WY.

Nestled within the Black Hills about ten miles northeast of Rapid City, South Dakota is Ellsworth Air Force Base. Constructed in 1941 and originally named Rapid City Army Air Base, the name was changed in 1953 to honor the late Brigadier General Richard Elmer Ellsworth.

Cheryl Lynn Carter

Sgt. Mario Anthony Woods, Jr. age 23 was stationed at Ellsworth AFB from 1975 to 1983 where he was a member of the 44th Missile Security Squadron. His job entailed the surveillance and protection of weapons; nuclear weapons such as the 150 Minuteman II missiles secretly hidden underground beneath the golden wheat fields.

The Minuteman, the first solid-fuel intercontinental Ballistic Missile, was one of the most significant strategic weapons in United States history, for with the turn of a key, these missiles could be launched to a Soviet Union target in less than fifteen minutes.

Minute Man Wings consist of three or four squadrons with each squadron comprised of five Missile Launch Facilities. Also known as Nuclear Silos, these include a vertical cylindrical underground structure for the storage and launching of intercontinental ballistic missiles. These facilities monitor the missiles from a 24/7 underground Launch Control Center. The structure is reinforced with steel and concrete strong enough to withstand any nuclear weapon attack.

Shortly before Thanksgiving in November 1977, Sgt. Woods was assigned to the Flight Control Facility as a member of the Security Response Team Novermber-1 working the night shift from 6:00 p.m. to 6:00 a.m. With him was Sgt. Michael Johnson who was working vacation relief. Having two months more seniority than Sgt. Woods, he was Team Leader during that shift.

Sgt. Mario Anthony Woods

It was a very cold night with temperatures around 9 degrees and light patches of snow on the ground. Sgt. Woods would occasionally step outside in order to stretch his legs, have a cigarette, and look up at the stars. At approximately 9:30 p.m. he observed a very bright light due east. It was different than the other stars and wasn't Venus or Jupiter. His first thought was that it was two B-52 Bombers flying in tandem at a low altitude. However, the more he watched its movement he came to realize it might have been a Black Hawk helicopter. Intrigued, for several minutes he continued to observe the object that he estimated was to be five miles away, as it hovered thirty degrees above the horizon.

Upon going back inside he mentioned the strange light in the sky to Sgt. Johnson who was sitting in the day room watching tv. However, he didn't think much of it at the time. Feeling it could be important, he decided to notify the Flight Security Controller that acted as a go-between for the Response Team and the Missile Capsule Crew Officers.

There was something about this that he couldn't get out of his mind. About thirty minutes later, he decided to step outside once more, but this time the object wasn't there. Thinking it must have been a helicopter after all, he started to walk back inside. However, suddenly the light appeared again at the same elevation, but more to the north. Then a thought crossed his mind. Why not flash the facility lights off and on as a means to communicate? The Flight Control Facility was equipped with fourteen sets of bright spotlights that were located at all four corners of the security perimeter fence as well as along the roofline of the building. These were all controlled by one switch in the Flight Security Controller's office.

Heading inside, he was eager to share his plan with SSgt. Bill Holliman who was talking to his wife on the phone. He nodded his head and waved him on. Still not certain if the object was something unusual or merely a helicopter, he reached for the switch and began to flash the lights in no particular sequence; on and off three times. Immediately, he received a response in the form of a flash.

He asked his team member Sgt. Johnson to walk outside while he flashed the lights again. The object flashed back. By now the object should have been getting closer and they should be hearing sound, but that didn't happen. After the flash, the object disappeared. Thinking it was probably a star Sgt. Johnson went back inside.

At 9:45, the object reappeared for a third time so he again began flashing the facility lights on and off three times and the object in turn flashed back. He related to the others that the object had reappeared and he was again experiencing intelligent interaction. Unfortunately, neither of them felt his light experiment was relative. This time when he went outside the elusive object was no longer visible. Thinking it had been a helicopter playing with him he thought to himself, "Well, I guess the show's over." Without giving it another thought, he went inside to the day room to watch tv before the three stations signed off at midnight.

Cheryl Lynn Carter

At 10:30 p.m. an emergency alert sounded in the office. The annoying sound wouldn't stop until the phone was answered. Upon answering, they received a Situation-4 Alert from Launch Flight November-5 located near the town of Newell, population 230, which meant outer and interior alarm activation.

After receiving their codes and a safety briefing from the Launch Control Center, they loaded their weapons and ditty bags containing extra clothing in case they had to spend the night, into the F-150 police vehicle, and began the 15 minute drive down Highway 79 toward November-5 with Sgt. Johnson driving. Upon arriving, they were to use their code to enter the gate and patrol around the inside perimeter of the fence. There was a three stage program: the above ground antenna array, the underground support building that helps control the humidity so the missiles don't overheat, and a six foot wide concrete barrier above it. During the winter, the entire site is buried under three to four feet of snow. If they needed to reset the alarms, they would have to shovel the snow.

On very rare occasions, should the missile start a sequence to launch that can't be overrode, Protocol in such a situation was to drive to the location, leave the vehicle in neutral above the silo hatch, and then run like Hell as far away to safety as possible. The vehicle would fall and destroy the gyro.

Sgt. Woods looked off into the distance where he observed a luminous object near the November-5 missile site about seven miles away and pointed it out to Sgt. Johnson. They did not radio in about the sighting, but continued on.

They turned down onto Orman Road that led to November-5. After turning left, the sky directly over the site was totally lit up as if it were daylight, illuminated by a sphere shape with gaseous colors of swirling red, orange, and white around the exterior. It was looming about ten feet above the ground and Sgt. Woods estimated it to be the width of a large warehouse.

They reached a cattle guard which was built into the ground and stopped at a forty-five degree angle to the gate. The luminous phenomenon, so massive that it dwarfed the site, was so bright as if the sun itself was sitting there. There was no sound, nor engines, and it was aeronautically unexplainable. The men sat there in a tactical position, but they were not at all prepared for this.

The atmosphere inside the truck became ionized, it felt as if the air was being vacuumed out, and time appeared to slow down. Sgt. Woods turned to see Sgt. Johnson bathed in a bluish light with both hands still on the steering wheel looking ahead with a blank stare on his face.

For some reason Sgt. Woods felt that he had to ask for relief of that pressure. Concerned for his safety, he didn't open the vehicle door. Instead, he rolled down the window, removed his right mitten, and picked up the maglite. With his right hand, he grabbed the large, stainless steel mirror on the side of the truck to pull himself out on the window sill. He grabbed the blue bubble light on the top of the truck with his left hand. Reaching across with his right hand, he began to flash the object in the same manner as he did at the Launch Control Facility.

As if his request was granted, a few seconds later, the heaviness dissipated and he was able to breathe normal again. Slinking down into his seat, he secured his M-16 between his knees. He looked over at Sgt. Johnson, his hands still on the steering wheel, to see him frozen, looking straight out the front window. The last thing he remembered was telling him that it was going to be all right before dropping his head and passing out.

Chosen

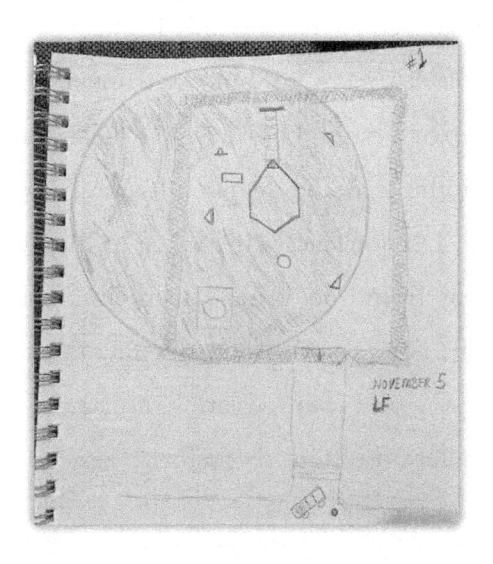

© Drawings from Sgt. Mario Woods sketchbook
Luminous phenomenon hovering over November-5
Large black sphere in front of the windshield
and beings on the driver's side

He managed to momentarily lift his head up and there was a huge black sphere bobbing in front of the windshield. It was the size of a beach ball, dent-like lines all over it, and in the middle nothing. As he dropped his head again, he heard, "Do not fear. Do not fear." He looked to the right and about ten feet away from the vehicle were little beings coming towards them. They stood about four feet tall, teal skin, large heads, big eyes, and were wearing little uniforms. Behind them was a taller one about six feet with large menacing eyes.

One of the small ones had a rod in his belt with a tip that looked like a pencil that was glowing a tangerine color. The tall one had something in the center of his chest about the size of the palm of a hand that was pulsating that same color. He became fixated on the light and even though the windows were up, he kept hearing, "Do not fear. Do not fear," as the sound traveled through every cell of his body like a vibration to his brain.

Chosen

© Drawings from Sgt. Mario Woods
Sketchbook of the beings

It felt like he was experiencing tunnel vision and then everything turned completely dark. He began questioning his mind and everything about his very existence ... everything. Images were quickly flashing in front of him; thoughts of his father, his mother, a total life review. He was fighting to keep his eyes open, but something was willing him to let go ... "Do not fear. Do not fear. We are not going to hurt you."

Moments later, he lifted his head up and realized he was on his back floating in the air three feet above the ground. Down below he could see the gold Air Force logo on the side of the truck door. As he tried to struggle, he felt a hand unlike any human hand grab his right shoulder and he passed out.

"What's your status?"

When he woke up, he was back inside the truck. A voice came over the radio saying, "November -1, what's your status?" He looked over at Sgt. Johnson asking him if he was going to get that, but he was still staring into space. He poked his shoulder with no reaction so he picked up the mic to respond. They asked, "Do you need help?" He said they did not. "Where are you located?"

Thinking that was a very odd response, he looked for Sgt. Johnson's reaction, but there was none. He asked Flight Security Control to hold on because for some reason the facility lights at November-5 were not on as they should be at night. However, upon stepping out of the vehicle he realized they were nowhere near the facility. Where were they? Even though it was only 9 degrees, the surrounding ground that should have been frozen solid was soft mud. A few feet to his right was a snow covered wall that was at a forty-five degree angle. About eight yards away he saw a lone tree in the middle of nowhere. Moreover, he did not see tire marks indicating they had driven there. It was as though the vehicle had been set down on the six foot wide road; a road where there was nowhere to turn a vehicle around.

Flight Control told him to wait as they were triangulating their position. Back-up was on their way. Twenty minutes later they arrived with Sgt. Garza and Sgt. Woods began asking questions as to what was going on. Had somebody taken care of November-5? However, they only remarked that they had been ordered not to discuss the situation. What situation?

Driving back to November-1 Control, Sgt. Woods took over because Sgt. Johnson still was unable to speak. He was astonished to discover that nearly five hours had passed during which time six Security Police Alert teams including the Flight Chief, Assistant, and two local deputies had been searching for them. Where had they been during that missing time and where was this place so unfamiliar to him? He was told that their vehicle was parked seven miles north of November -5. The wall covered with snow, was the dam that held the water of Newell Lake. They had been parked on a six foot wide runoff. Had Sgt. Johnson opened his driver's door to step out, he would have fallen down an incline to a huge frozen lake below.

Back at the Facility, the men were separated. Sgt. Johnson was still not communicating, but able to walk with assistance. He was taken to the day room where he was being attended by medical staff. Sgt. Woods was taken to the Wing Commander's office to be questioned. During the interview there were several present including Col. Spraker, the Assistant Base Commander, two OSI Office of Special Investigation officers Captain Jack Reed with Richard Doty being an observer, and a tall man in a dark suit wearing a hat.

"I felt like I was leaving my body!"

He was questioned for a half hour before asking to use the bathroom. Once inside, he sat on the toilet in the second stall with his full uniform on trying to decompress. A green light surrounded him followed by the sensation that he was leaving his physical body. He could feel his soul travel down from his head to the point of separation at his feet. Somehow he knew he had a clear channel to do that. Thankfully, the sound of a K-9 entering the room and the voice of somebody asking if he was okay relieved him of the strange feeling. He went over to the sink, splashed cold water on his face, and was escorted back to the office.

Once there, he was interviewed for two additional hours, although he felt it was more of an interrogation. Then the two OSI officers and the man in the suit escorted him to the base hospital. Once again Richard Doty was only present to observe. The doctor conducted the usual examination and noticed there were burns on the right side of Sgt. Woods face and the back of his right hand. This was most likely caused by the bright light. He had been wearing his beret and holding the maglite in his right hand. After taking skin samples from his forehead and hand, the doctor put them into vials and set them on a silver tray. The doctor also noticed two pock marks, one on his inner left ankle and the other under his left arm. He was never given the results of his exam.

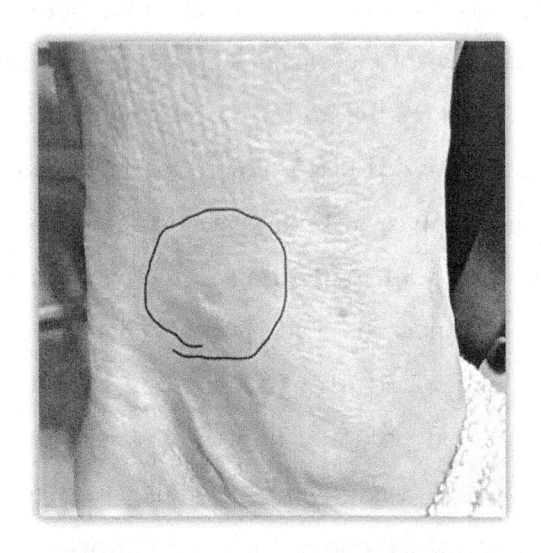

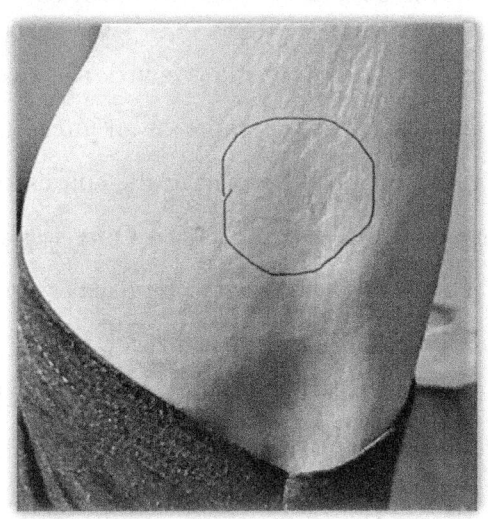

© Sgt. Mario Woods -Pock marks on inner
left ankle and under left arm

Chosen

The men drove him back to the office where he was required to write an incident report. The report with the word "UFO" at the top was three carbon pages thick and needed to be filled out with a number two pen. For an hour and twenty minutes he related what happened that night beginning at November-1 up until the glowing light over November-5. He made no mention as to what he observed outside the window. Afterwards, he was required to sign a Non-Disclosure Agreement known as a Personal Reliability Clause.

When he returned home after receiving an extra day off, he was not able to even explain what was happening to his wife. Failure to comply would result in them removing him from his position and sending him somewhere he wouldn't want to be. Nonetheless, when he returned to work, he was transferred to the Key Low Control an alternate command post. There he would work with Supervisor Mark Wade, an Assistant Supervisor, and a Team Leader that had only two weeks more seniority than him. A few months later he received orders to be sent to Korea for a 14 month tour most likely to ensure he would have no contact with anyone involved that night.

Two weeks after the incident, Sgt. Johnson knocked on the door of his home. They sat down and talked for two hours; more than they had ever done that first night during their shift. Sgt. Woods asked him if he could draw the object they encountered. Then sitting in opposite rooms, they drew what they had seen at the November-5 gate with identical results. Sgt. Johnson also remembered hearing, "Do not fear. Do not fear." He told Sgt. Woods, "I remember your mitten on a shiny floor." Surprised by that comment, he went over to get his diddy bag and dumped it out on the couch. Only the left glove was there. That was the last time they spoke.

Sgt. Woods contends that the incident will always be a part of him. He would have strange dreams of earthquakes, tidal waves, atomic blasts, and developed an interest in pyramids, mathematical designs, and archeology. He was inclined to get a map and measure the distances between November-1, the Newell Dam, and November-5, where he discovered it to be an equilateral triangle.

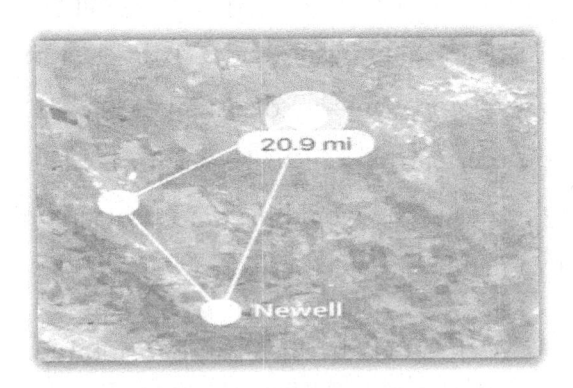

Hypnotic Regression
January, 22, 2016

Hypnotist: "As you're laying there totally relaxed, your mind starts to wander. And it goes back to the time that you were in the military. Before anything happens you're sitting in the patrol vehicle. What happens next?'

Mario: "I was afraid to leave the vehicle. I should have stepped out, but I couldn't."

Hypnotist: "It's okay, you're safe now, Mario. We're just looking at a movie. Take a deep breath and pause the picture. So how many are there?"

Mario: "Four and a tall one behind them."

Hypnotist: "So how tall was the tall one?"

Mario: "Six foot maybe."

Hypnotist: "Can you describe him?"

Mario: "Yes, he had a long head. He had a very long head. When he looked at me, he just looked right through me. The little guys didn't bother me like he did."

Hypnotist: "What's around you now?"

Mario: "I'm in some type of room, some kind of inspection area. They're just checking me. And then I ask, 'Where's Michael?' And they told me not to worry about it. I see that big tall bastard and he's looking at me ... looking. ... I don't like this guy. He has a uniform on that has creases in it like a ranking officer or something. It's this tall guy ... is really not a ... not a good person. I feel a pinch on my lower left side now. It's like somebody got a hold on me or something. And it's fast and it's not kind."

Interview with Linda Moulton Howe, Investigative Journalist

Mario: "It's Orman Road and we turned right at the stop sign. You know I couldn't wait to see it. I was kind of excited and scared to see it at the same time. We go down about a mile, a mile and a quarter and that hard top road drops off into clay, and dog-legs off to the left. And Linda, as he dog-legged that corner, this object was sitting on top of November-5. It looked like a mini sun. And honestly the only comparison I've said to people was it was the size of a Super Walmart Center sitting ten feet off the ground right over

November-5. And it was so bright as if it was the sun sitting there."

Linda: "Did it have color?"

Mario: "Yes, it was red, orange, and white. There were no hard edges, no surface features that I could see. There were no wings. There were no portals or areas of propulsion. There was nothing like that whatsoever. We rolled up to the cattle gate which is built in the ground not a gate you have to open and we stopped there at a forty-five degree angle like we were going to do something. What could we do literally? We sat right at the end of that cattle gate road in a tactical position both frozen in what we were doing. We just couldn't move. The light got so bright I could almost see it through my hands it was so bright. I had to close my eyes because the dashboard, everything in that vehicle was lit up just like that movie 'Close Encounters of the Third Kind' that mailbox scene. It was like that.

Then the atmosphere started evacuating after. The light never stopped. And all of a sudden, we couldn't breathe and it was if somebody sucked all the air out of the cab of that truck. I've never experienced anything like it. The only thing I could do to get relief, and I knew I had to ask, was I rolled down that passenger window of that F150 Ford pickup truck, dark blue USAF Security Police on the side of it in letters. We had those stainless steel, western style, large mirrors on the side of our truck and I took my maglite and I pulled myself with my right hand out on to the window sill of that vehicle. And why I did that I don't know, but I grabbed the blue bubbles that were on top of the vehicle with my left hand, and I had a mitten on and I reached across with my right hand, and I flashed this object with the same sequence I guess that I did at the LCF with my maglite. And I did that a couple times.

In my mind I was asking for relief of this pressure, whatever it was I can't describe, and then I just slinked down into this seat. And I'm a pretty good sized fellow in pretty good shape. I remember putting my weapon between my knees. I knew I had to secure it for some reason. I don't know where my flashlight went, but I just dropped my head and I was out. My last thing was I looked at Michael Johnson and he was frozen looking straight ahead on the steering wheel looking straight out the front window.

I guess I lifted my head up a couple of times and I had seen this black sphere bobbing in front of the truck like a beach ball. But it had all these little dents all over it like it was in layers. It was like a beach ball with lines on it and in the middle there was nothing there."

Linda: "Not glowing any light?"

Mario: "All black and I just remember that bobbing in front of the windshield real fast, real quick. As I dropped my head, I kept sensing or feeling something, 'Do not fear. Do not fear.' And I just rotated my head to the right as if I was in tunnel vision and I see these little beings about ten feet away from the vehicle coming toward me and they've got little uniforms on. They had large heads, but not over size, but they did have big eyes. Behind them was a tall one and he was more menacing. That's the one I centered on and I felt fear from that one.

Linda: "What did you see in the tall one?"

Mario: "Well, large eyes, just a bigger, meaner rendition of the two that were in front of him by a couple of feet. He was like coming up behind them. He was probably about two feet taller than the ones in front of him. "

Linda: "What would be the height of the small and the large?"

Mario: "The tall one maybe 5 ½ or 6 foot and the ones in front of him maybe 4 or 4 ½."

Linda: "And what color uniforms were the small ones in?"

Mario: "They were in like a grey uniform. The one of the right, he had a belt. And on the one on the left, he had this rod in his belt that had a tip that looked like a pencil, but it was glowing, and it was glowing yellow."

Linda: "Did he grab it in his hand?"

Mario: "I never saw that, but the one behind him had something in the center of his chest. It was pulsating that same glow, that same color. It was the size of your palm in the middle of his chest and it had a glow to it growing brighter and dimmer."

Linda: "What color on Earth would match color of the glow from the taller being's chest?"

Mario: "A cross between orange and white … tangerine perhaps."

Linda: "Was it glowing with a whitish light?"

Mario: "Yes, with a whitish light. And it wasn't super bright, it was dull, but with that tint. When I looked at that and kept hearing, 'Do not fear. Do not fear,' it was not words I was hearing because the windows were up. It was inside of me as if it was in water or something coming through me. I could hear it inside my ear drums without any noise from outside whatsoever."

Linda: "Thoughts were inside your own mind. What was the tall one wearing?"

Mario: "He had on a similar uniform, but it was different. It was belted and it was more of a darker grey color, but it was hard to look at anything else but the eyes. The face of the tall one was different than the face of the two smaller ones. The face of the tall one was more of a rugged, more threatening type of look. Cheek bones were different, raised higher, entire jaw line was much thinner, and protruded differently than the smaller ones that had more rounded features even though they had larger eyes. I can't remember the exact length of their arms because as they walked their arms were directly at their side. Their hands were in front of them and their hands were three fingers and a thumb."

Linda: "Did the taller one have scales like a Reptilian?"

Mario: "No, did not. And the skin color wasn't grey. It was more like a teal."

Linda: "And we now have drawings of these teal blue beings that existed back in 1977 even if people weren't saying they were looking at teal blue beings."

Mario: "Wow, I had no idea."

Linda: "Now as you were passing out, what happened inside?"

Mario: "It was as if I'm in tunnel vision and I'm allowed to see what I'm seeing. Because I remember going completely dark and questioning my mind and everything about my existence ... EVER ... everything. I mean it all flashes in front of you like thoughts of my father, my mother ... Just everything that was happening, it all came to me in one flash."

Linda: "Mario, are you saying you had something like a life review sitting in that military truck with this gigantic UFO, and these extraterrestrial biological entities approaching you, that you were given through your mind's eye like a movie of a life review?"

Mario: "I never looked at it that way, but yes it had to be. Really it just shook me to my core. It was so fast and I didn't think a thought could move that fast. It was just so strange to have this tunnel vision as if I was fighting to not close my eyes, but yet somehow being told to close my eyes. And I kept hearing, 'Do not fear. Do not fear. We are not going to hurt you,' over and over again."

Linda: "Today in September 2021 as we are talking, do you have any more evolved information or knowledge about why the tall being and the shorter beings would have run through your life in your mind's eye at Ellsworth AFB when they had a huge UFO over a missile site?"

Mario: "I really don't know. It was just being either at the right place at the wrong time or the wrong place at the right time. It did not end there and it continued on."

Linda: "What happened?"

Mario: "Well, I have memories. I remember somehow or another they got me out of that truck. I was on my back and I remember lifting up my head three or four feet above the ground as if I was on a stretcher being moved or something. I still have no contact or thoughts of Michael Johnson knowing that he was in that vehicle still staring forward with this blank stare in his eyes. And the next thing that I remember is being in something dark and cold. It felt like a Jell-o or something. I felt completely alone and had no idea where or what was going on. And a feeling of dread came upon me and it really, really, really upset me."

Linda: "What was the next thing you remembered?"

Mario: "A white wall …That white wall, I didn't know this at the time, I'd never been there before was the backside of the Newell Lake Reservoir Dam that's north of Newell and about eleven miles away from November-5. And I had no idea what this white wall was. Well, low and behold the backside of that reservoir goes down about forty to fifty feet. As you get closer to the edge, the edge goes up ten to twenty feet and then you're on level ground. It's a great big huge berm on the backside of that Newell Lake Reservoir and we were at the bottom of that sitting on it. Had we driven down in there, there's no place to turn around because there's about a fifty foot drop-off into another lake that's a run-off area for that dam. There's nowhere to turn a vehicle around."

Linda: "It would have never been possible for you to have driven your military vehicle there in November of 1977?"

Mario: "That is correct. Still couldn't do it today. There's no way that a vehicle could turn around down there because it's just straight down off to the side to your right."

Linda: "The implication is that the teal, bluish beings transported you out of the military vehicle you were in with Michael Johnson. Do you have any insights now about why the entities would have transported you to that narrow place in the reservoir?"

Mario: "Yes. I believe that when I first spotted that craft when I walked out of November-1 Launch Control Facility that night, I believe they were directly above it or right next to the Newell Reservoir Dam itself. I don't know what they would be doing there, but as the crow flies that was where about they were located. And it was as if they took me to a point where I first observed them."

Linda: "And that was the flashing of the lights where all this started and you thought it was a joke with some helicopter pilots."

Mario: "Yes, ma'am and why I used that maglite to ask for relief for what was happening to me. I just think they were the ones sent because that craft was much larger of only holding three beings. That craft was filled with stuff and I've had dreams since that about the inside of that thing."

Linda: "What did you dream?"

Mario: "I dreamt I'd been in a room with all kind of artifacts from Earth like box tvs, old radios, and antennas all this stuff sitting up on shelves. The first thing I saw was an old b&w box television set probably a 19x19 something like that with the knobs on the right side of the cabinet and the old style wood grain that was plastic and I put my hand on it. Next to it was a sewing machine, an IBM typewriter, below it, a radio, a pedestal kind of light that people used to put from the floor to the ceiling. All this stuff was extremely old and I just found it fascinating to be where I was. I was like, oh wow, you got one of these."

Linda: "You are describing that you saw in some type of dream or in your mind's eye a section inside this craft that was filled with 20th Century human technology. Did you ask any of them in your mind what is this for and why have you taken me?"

Mario: "No, I said why do you have all this old stuff? I remember saying that. I don't believe I got an answer. They had me come with them down this hallway and that's when I noticed the walls that were so active with circuits and lights. I didn't fear at the time. I was amazed at the things that I saw there. I mean there was some really strange old stuff that we've used all of our lives, you know? "

Linda: "Like archeologists from another planet came here and they were stuffing the UFO with technologies to study."

Mario: "They did tell me when they took me there that I could look out the window. And I was afraid to look out the window because I was afraid of what I would be looking at …the Earth or something? I really wish I would have now. I only know that in that room I did not feel fear. The only time I felt fear was when I was having a lot of pain in my right wrist. I can still feel that pain in my wrist today. I don't know why."

Linda: "Have you ever been given an insight from your dreams about why they, the non-humans would be taking technologies from the 20th Century? And why they were there near Ellsworth AFB interacting with you and Michael Johnson?"

Mario: "I don't know. When I followed them, I kept looking at things as I'm walking out of that room because I found it so interesting because it was things that I had interfaced with. Coming out of this room I don't remember a door, but I remember a short hallway. The hallway was really tall, about six to eight feet wide, but really tall. We turned left and there was a doorway that was already opened when I got there. As I looked in it was like fog in the whole area and I was in the fog too. It felt like somebody took me by the hand and when I looked up, I saw this gargantuan interior that was multi-layered like the whole interior of this craft had rooms. These little guys were everywhere."

Linda: "Do you think that what the beings were trying to do was communicate to you that we have gathered this from you, from your planet, and that they maybe are awaiting a reaction from you about these? But the bottom line is, they are basically communicating we study your planet. We gather from your planet. You are now on our craft and we are now showing you some of what we have taken from your planet and you, we have taken from your planet ... What do you think the tall and short teal blue beings want from Earth and from humans?"

Mario: "I think the tall beings are the ones with the true mission and knowledge of what their mission is on this planet and who they are trying to please. The short beings are simply the ones that carry out what they want done. I don't think the short ones can grow up to be tall ones. I think they are two different species. I think they are symbiotic. You don't see one without the other. Maybe they're protectors. I honestly don't know."

Linda: "What do they want from Earth and humans?"

Mario: "I believe understanding. I think they want to know what makes us tick, what makes us warring, maybe our inner most thoughts, our inner most fears, our inner most everything. Because I do think they can separate the mind or the soul from the body and analyze it in a way that we can't even imagine."

Testifies to the Pentagon UFO Program – AARO

On May 14, 2023, he received an email from AARO, All-Domain Anomaly Resolution Office inquiring if he would consider testifying in front of the Pentagon. AARO, preceded by AATIP, the Advanced Aerospace Threat Identification Program, was established in 2022.

Under the direction of Dr. Sean M. Kirkpatrick, its Mission is to synchronize efforts across the Department of Defense, and with other U.S. Federal Agencies, to detect, identify, and attribute objects of interest in, on, or near military installations, operating areas, special use airspace, and other areas of interest to mitigate any associated threats to safety of operations and national security. This includes anomalous, unidentified space, airborne, submerged, and transmedium objects.

While under oath, he testified to the Pentagon's AARO during a four hour audio interview. He detailed his UFO experience while he was deployed at the 44th Missile Security Squadron in 1977. Beforehand he was instructed about security measures concerning exactly what information he could or could not disclose.

Cheryl Lynn Carter

> OSD Pentagon OUSD Intel - Sec Mailbox
> AARO-External
>
> Invitation for an Interview with AARO
> Mar 14, 2023 at 5:00:49 PM
>
> Mr. Woods,
>
> The All-domain Anomaly Resolution Office (AARO), Office of the Under Secretary of Defense for Intelligence and Security (OUSD (I&S)) is conducting oral history interviews----consistent with Congressional direction----as an opportunity to incorporate into the official record discrete knowledge and experiences of those exposed to the US Government's previous Unidentified Anomalous Phenomena (UAP) investigations. Any information provided during the interview will be secured in accordance with the Government's strict security and privacy requirements, including----consistent with any previous NDAs.
>
> We value the historical information you may have on persons, activities, and events of US UAP investigations, and we welcome your participation in the interview. Your privacy is paramount, and the interview would be held discreetly in a secure location. Any discussion in a secure facility with AARO is deemed by the classification control office of both the DoD (SAPCO) and ODNI (CAPCO) an authorized disclosure, and you can speak freely.
>
> It is important to note that the purpose of the interview is not to collect information about you, but rather, gather historical information you may have regarding sensitive government programs and any potential nexus to unidentified anomalies.
>
> Please let us know whether you have interest in participating in this secure, protected, and historical interview.
>
> The AARO Team

Invitation for an interview from AARO

Chosen

Dr. Sean M. Kirkpatrick made a statement during a briefing, "There is no correlation with UFOs and nuclear weapons."

Sgt. Mario Woods reply, "With all your resources, scientific background, and what you know, if you think that this is not going on you're mistaken. And you need to come to grips with it because it has happened to people. And by God … it happened to ME!"

© Earthfiles: September 29, 2021 – America's Minuteman Nuclear Missile Program Has Been Haunted By UFOs – Part 1 and 2

September 29, 2021 - America's Minuteman Nuclear Missile Program Has Been Haunted by UFOs. - YouTube

October 6, 2021 - Part 2: America's Minuteman Nuclear Missile Program Has Been Haunted by UFOs. - YouTube

Cheryl Lynn Carter

The Edge of Enigma

Being witness to glimpses of other realities can have a profound effect on the mind. Our emotions inherently express how we react to each situation. While some emotions leave us feeling good, others might cause one to mentally compartmentalize the entire experience burying it deeply within the echoes of their psyche where it would remain suppressed forever. Perhaps it is because a person finds the experience too difficult to process or feels it is deemed socially unacceptable to share. After all, what is it like carrying the weight of a mystery?

Time moves on, but a person cannot escape what they never left behind. Something instills in them a feeling of duality with the non-human intelligence that allowed them to become privy to unprecedented knowledge. Knowledge that it is possible the past, present, and future are intrinsically one. Being chosen, they have become witness to another world. To them it is evident that we will always be connected to the other-worldly ones that have been shaping both our history and future traversing the space-time continuum.

Made in the USA
Columbia, SC
13 August 2024